This Book Belongs To

Start Planning Your Trip To Minnesota

Minnesota is a picturesque Midwestern town that borders both Canada and Lake Superior. Minnesota's proximity to these awesome places makes it all the more special to visit. Nicknamed The Gopher State, Minnesota is loaded with history, culture, and nature by the mile.

With 10,000 lakes, remarkable ecosystems, wilderness preserves, hundreds of state parks, and nature conservatories to name a few, it's no wonder visitors come from all over just to bask in the state's natural wonders.

If you're planning an upcoming trip to The Gopher State, you're definitely looking for cool things to do in Minnesota. Thankfully, you won't have to look far because places to visit in MN are plenty. Minnesota is home to museums, amusement parks, incredible shopping, historic estates, distilleries, and so much more.

Whether you're researching things to do in Minnesota to keep you active and outdoors or indoors observing cultural institutions, there are countless awesome places to visit in MN.

From tons of state parks to camping destinations for days and shopping for the books to museums by the mile, MN is a wonderful place to spend time with family and friends. No matter what draws you to The Gopher State, there's something to do for everyone.

Come to MN for its natural beauty and outdoor recreation, stay for its history and culture, and leave having fulfilled a lifetime's worth of amazing experiences.

Happy Adventure.

Your feedback means a lot for us!

Please, Consider leaving us "5 stars" on your
Amazon review.
Thank You!

L.P	PLACES TO GO	LOCATION	EST.	VISITED
1	MINNESOTA'S NORTH SHORE SCENIC DRIVE	MINNESOTA U.S	....	
2	MINNEAPOLIS INSTITUTE OF ART	MINNEAPOLIS	1883	
3	COMO PARK ZOO & CONSERVATORY	ST PAUL	1873	
4	GREAT LAKES AQUARIUM	DULUTH	2000	
5	INTERNATIONAL WOLF CENTER	ELY	1993	
6	THE FREDERICK R. WEISMAN ART MUSEUM	MINNEAPOLIS	1934	
7	THE HISTORIC CONGDON ESTATE	DULUTH	1908	
8	JAMES J. HILL HOUSE	ST PAUL	1891	
9	SPLIT ROCK LIGHTHOUSE	TWO HARBORS	1969	
10	ROCKFILTER DISTILLERY	SPRING GROVE	....	
11	MINNESOTA HISTORY CENTER	ST PAUL	1992	
12	LAKE SUPERIOR MARINE MUSEUM	DULUTH	1973	
13	MINNEAPOLIS SCULPTURE GARDEN	MINNEAPOLIS	1988	
14	NORTH AMERICAN BEAR CENTER	ELY	....	
15	SCIENCE MUSEUM OF MINNESOTA	ST PAUL	1907	
16	MILL CITY MUSEUM	MINNEAPOLIS	2003	
17	7 VINES VINEYARD	DELLWOOD	2012	
18	NATIONAL EAGLE CENTER	WABASHA	1995	
19	MINNESOTA LANDSCAPE ARBORETUM	CHASKA	1958	
20	LEIF ERICKSON PARK & ROSE GARDEN	DULUTH	1965	
21	MINNEHAHA PARK	MINNEAPOLIS	1885	
22	QUARRY HILL NATURE CENTER	ROCHESTER	....	
23	SUPERIOR NATIONAL FOREST	DULUTH	1909	
24	VOYAGEURS NATIONAL PARK	INTERNATIONAL FALLS	1975	
25	MALL OF AMERICA	BLOOMINGTON	1992	
26	MUNSINGER / CLEMENS GARDENS	ST CLOUD	1995	
27	THE AERIAL LIFT BRIDGE	DULUTH	1905	
28	ITASCA STATE PARK	PARK RAPIDS	1891	
29	CATHEDRAL OF ST. PAUL	ST PAUL	1915	
30	TETTEGOUCHE STATE PARK	SILVER BAY	1979	
31	GOOSEBERRY FALLS STATE PARK	TWO HARBORS	1937	
32	NICKELODEON UNIVERSE	BLOOMINGTON	1992	
33	MINNESOTA ZOO	APPLE VALLEY	1978	
34	SPAM MUSEUM	AUSTIN	1991	
35	THEODORE WIRTH REGIONAL PARK	GOLDEN VALLEY	1889	
36	SEA LIFE	BLOOMINGTON	1996	
37	STONE ARCH BRIDGE	MINNEAPOLIS	1883	
38	BOUNDARY WATERS CANOE AREA WILDERNESS	DULUTH	1978	
39	NIAGARA CAVE	HARMONY	1934	
40	TEMPERANCE RIVER	SCHROEDER	....	
41	LAKE MINNETONKA	MINNESOTA U.S	....	
42	PIPESTONE NATIONAL MONUMENT	PIPESTONE	1937	
43	MUSEUM OF QUESTIONABLE MEDICAL DEVICES	SAINT PAUL	....	
44	MINNESOTA'S LARGEST CANDY STORE	JORDAN	....	
45	BEAR HEAD LAKE STATE PARK	ELY	1961	
46	BLUE MOUNDS STATE PARK	LUVERNE	1937	
47	CASCADE RIVER STATE PARK	LUTSEN	1957	
48	FRONTENAC STATE PARK	FRONTENAC	1957	
49	GLACIAL LAKES STATE PARK	STARBUCK	1963	
50	GRAND PORTAGE STATE PARK	GRAND PORTAGE	1989	

Inventory

☐ Binoculars	☐ Sport Shoes
☐ Bear Spray	☐ Swim Wear
☐ Cell Phone + Charger	☐ Towel
☐ Camera + Accessories	☐ Rainproof Backpack Cover
☐ First aid kit	☐ Pendrive
☐ Flashlight / Headlamp	☐ Powerbank
☐ Fleece / Waterproof Jacket	☐ Laptop
☐ Guide Book	☐ Small Tripod
☐ Hand Lotion	☐ Phone Holder
☐ Hiking Shoes	☐ Extender Cable
☐ Hand Sanitizer	☐ Bulbs / Fuses
☐ Insect Repellent	☐ Scissors
☐ Lip Balm	☐ Tent
☐ Medications & Painkillers	☐ Trash Bags
☐ Maps	☐ Umbrella
☐ Ticket / Pass	☐ National Park Maps
☐ Snacks	☐ National Park Maps
☐ Sunglasses	☐ Cosmetics
☐ Spare Socks	☐ Passport / Photocopy
☐ Sunscreen	☐ Id Card
☐ Sun Hat	☐ Driver's License
☐ Trash Bags	☐ ATM Cards
☐ Toilet Paper	☐ Cash
☐ Walking Stick	☐ Green Card
☐ Water	☐ Tool Box

Minnesota's North Shore Scenic Drive

VISTED DATE :   SPRING ◯   SUMMER ◯   FALL ◯   WINTER ◯

WEATHER :   ☀ ◯   ⛅ ◯   🌧 ◯   🌨 ◯   ⛈ ◯   🌬 ◯   🌡 TEMP :

FEE(S) :   RATING : ☆ ☆ ☆ ☆ ☆   WILL I RETURN?   YES / NO

LODGING :   WHO I WENT WITH :

DESCRIPTION / THINGS TO DO :

ONE OF THE BEST WAYS TO EXPLORE MINNESOTA IS BY CRUISING THE NORTH SHORE SCENIC DRIVE.

OF NOTE, THIS SCENIC DESTINATION IS DESIGNATED AN "ALL AMERICAN ROAD" ALONG WHICH YOU CAN ENJOY THE PICTURESQUE SCENERY OF THE NORTH SHORE OF LAKE SUPERIOR.

ALONG THE SPECTACULAR ROUTE, YOU WILL ENCOUNTER PLENTY OF PLACES TO SEE, ESPECIALLY TOURIST ATTRACTIONS.

ASTOUNDINGLY, YOU'LL ENCOUNTER A WHOPPING EIGHT STATE PARKS, ANY OF WHICH MAKES A GREAT PIT STOP FOR EXPLORATION.

ADDITIONALLY, THERE ARE MANY QUAINT RESTAURANTS, UNIQUE SHOPS, AND ART GALLERIES TO CHECK OUT ALONG THE SCENIC DRIVE.

FURTHERMORE, BEYOND THE MANY SCENIC OVERLOOKS, YOU CAN ENJOY MANY HISTORICAL SIGHTS.

A FEW OF THE AMAZING HISTORICAL SIGHTS INCLUDE SPLIT ROCK LIGHTHOUSE, GRAND PORTAGE NATIONAL MONUMENT, AND THE GRAND MARAIS ART CENTER.

WITH SO MANY WONDERFUL THINGS TO DO IN MINNESOTA, THIS TOP ATTRACTION IS A MUST SEE.

ADDRESS: MN, UNITED STATES

PASSPORT STAMPS:

NOTES :

Minneapolis Institute of Art

VISTED DATE :   SPRING ◯ SUMMER ◯ FALL ◯ WINTER ◯

WEATHER : ☀ ◯ ⛅ ◯ 🌧 ◯ 🌨 ◯ ⛈ ◯ 💨 ◯   🌡 TEMP :

FEE(S) :   RATING : ☆ ☆ ☆ ☆ ☆   WILL I RETURN? YES / NO

LODGING :   WHO I WENT WITH :

DESCRIPTION / THINGS TO DO :

SITUATED IN THE HEART OF MINNEAPOLIS, MINNESOTA, THE MINNEAPOLIS INSTITUTE OF ART IS HOME TO NEARLY 100,000 WORKS OF ART AND ARTIFACTS THAT DEPICT 5,000 YEARS OF WORLD HISTORY.

ONE OF THE LARGEST MUSEUMS IN THE UNITED STATES, THE MINNEAPOLIS INSTITUTE OF ART FEATURES EXHIBITS OF CONTEMPORARY ART, MASTERPIECES, VISUAL ART, AND SO MUCH MORE.

SOME OF THE MUSEUM'S FEATURED EXHIBITS INCLUDE ENVISIONING EVIL: "THE NAZI DRAWINGS," SIXTIES PSYCHEDELIA, AND AMERICAN DOCUMENTARY PHOTOGRAPHY AMONG MANY OTHERS.

ONE OF MINNESOTA'S GREATEST TOURIST ATTRACTIONS, A VISIT TO THE MINNEAPOLIS INSTITUTE OF ART IS A MUST DO.

SIGNIFICANTLY, VISITING THE MUSEUM IS FREE FOR ALL AND REQUIRES NO ADVANCED RESERVATIONS.

DURING YOUR VISIT TO THIS TOP 10 DESTINATION, YOU CAN PLAN TO BROWSE LOADS OF ART EXHIBITS OR PARTICIPATE IN ONE OF MANY AWESOME MUSEUM PROGRAMS SUCH AS A CURATORIAL PROGRAM, CHILDREN'S EVENTS, AND OTHERS.

ONE OF MINNESOTA'S MOST POPULAR PLACES TO SEE, THE MINNEAPOLIS MUSEUM OF ART DESERVES A SPOT ON YOUR ITINERARY.

ADDRESS: 2400 3RD AVE S, MINNEAPOLIS, MN 55404, UNITED STATES

PASSPORT STAMPS:

NOTES :

Como Park Zoo and Conservatory

VISTED DATE :   SPRING ◯   SUMMER ◯   FALL ◯   WINTER ◯

WEATHER :   ☀◯   ⛅◯   ☁◯   🌨◯   ⛈◯   🌬◯   🌡 TEMP :

FEE(S) :   RATING : ☆ ☆ ☆ ☆ ☆   WILL I RETURN?   YES / NO

LODGING :   WHO I WENT WITH :

DESCRIPTION / THINGS TO DO :

LOCATED IN SAINT PAUL, MINNESOTA'S CAPITAL CITY, COMO PARK ZOO & CONSERVATORY IS ONE OF MANY AWESOME PLACES TO VISIT IN MN.

OPEN 365 DAYS A YEAR, COMO PARK ZOO & CONSERVATORY IS A TOP PLACE TO VISIT TODAY, TOMORROW, OR THIS WEEKEND.

COMO PARK ZOO & CONSERVATORY IS AN EXCELLENT PLACE TO SPEND THE DAY LEARNING AND EXPERIE-NCING UNIQUE WILDLIFE.

WITH THE HOPE OF INSPIRING A VALUE AND APPRECIATION FOR ALL LIVING THINGS, THE ZOO PROVIDES EXCELLENT EXHIBITS AND PROGRAMMING.

GO TO COMO PARK ZOO & CONSERVATORY TO CHECK OUT ANIMALS FROM ALL OVER THE WORLD.

YOU'LL HAVE THE OPPORTUNITY TO INTERACT WITH ANIMALS SUCH AS A GALAPAGOS TORTOISE AND AN ARCTIC FOX AND EVERYTHING IN BETWEEN.

IN ADDITION TO ALL OF THE AWESOME ANIMALS YOU'LL ENCOUNTER, THE ZOO IS ALSO HOME TO MANY BEAUTIFULLY DESIGNED GARDENS, ART EXHIBITS, AND EXCITING CHILDREN'S ATTRACTIONS.

LASTLY, SIGHTSEEING AND ENTERTAINMENT GO HAND IN HAND AT COMO PARK ZOO & CONSERVATORY SO BE SURE TO CHECK IT OUT WHEN PASSING THROUGH MINNESOTA.

ADDRESS: 1225 ESTABROOK DR, ST PAUL, MN 55103, UNITED STATES

PASSPORT STAMPS:

NOTES :

Great Lakes Aquarium

DESCRIPTION / THINGS TO DO :

SITUATED ON THE PICTURESQUE DULUTH WATERFRONT, GREAT LAKES AQUARIUM IS ONE OF MANY AWESOME PLACES TO VISIT IN MINNESOTA.

HAVING OPENED IN 2000, THIS NON-PROFIT ORGANIZATION HAS TONS OF LOVELY SEA LIFE TO OBSERVE. MOST NOTABLY, THE AQUARIUM PAYS CLOSE ATTENTION TO WILDLIFE AND HABITATS FOUND IN THE GREAT LAKES BASIN AND EVEN THE AMAZON RIVER.

GREAT LAKES AQUARIUM IS A FAMILY-FRIENDLY DESTINATION THAT TEACHES VISITORS ABOUT FRESHWATER ECOSYSTEMS.

WITH SO MUCH TO DO IN ONE PLACE, YOU'LL NEVER WONDER WHAT TO SEE NEXT WHEN VISITING THE GREAT LAKES AQUARIUM.

GREAT LAKES AQUARIUM IS HOME TO MANY SPECTACULAR EXHIBITS THAT SHOWCASE THE SEA LIFE OF THE REGION.

SOME OF THE MANY AMAZING EXHIBITS INCLUDE AQUATIC INVADERS, CRITTER CORNER, WATERSHEDS AT WORK, AND SHIPWRECKS ALIVE AMONG MANY MORE.

IN ADDITION TO THE MANY WONDERFUL AQUATIC EXHIBITS, THE ESTABLISHMENT IS ALSO HOME TO A FINE ARTS GALLERY WITH WORKS DEPICTING AQUATIC THEMES. WITH SO MANY THINGS TO SEE IN ONE BEAUTIFUL PLACE, IT'S NO WONDER TRAVELERS COME TO THE AQUARIUM FROM FAR AND WIDE.

ADDRESS: 353 HARBOR DR #100, DULUTH, MN 55802, UNITED STATES

PASSPORT STAMPS:

NOTES :

International Wolf Center

VISTED DATE :   SPRING ○   SUMMER ○   FALL ○   WINTER ○

WEATHER : ☀○ ⛅○ 🌧○ 🌨○ ⛈○ 🌬○   🌡TEMP :

FEE(S) :   RATING : ☆ ☆ ☆ ☆ ☆   WILL I RETURN?   YES / NO

LODGING :   WHO I WENT WITH :

DESCRIPTION / THINGS TO DO :

IF YOU'RE LOOKING FOR UNIQUE THINGS TO DO IN MN, BE SURE TO CHECK OUT THE INTERNATIONAL WOLF CENTER.

LOCATED IN ELY, MINNESOTA, THE CENTER IS A RESEARCH AND EDUCATIONAL FACILITY, OPENED TO THE PUBLIC, THAT PROMOTES THE "SURVIVAL OF WOLF POPULATIONS" AND THE ROLES AMERICANS PLAY IN ACHIEVING THAT GOAL.

BY EDUCATING VISITORS ABOUT THE PROBLEMS WOLVES FACE, PROBLEMS CAUSED BY HUMANITY, THE CENTER HOPES TO THWART PRACTICES DETRIMENTAL TO THE SPECIES.

DURING A VISIT TO THE INTERNATIONAL WOLF CENTER, VISITORS WILL LEARN ABOUT THE DIFFERENCES IN WOLVES AROUND THE WORLD AS WELL AS MEET A LIVE WOLF EXHIBIT.

CURRENTLY, THE PACK INCLUDES THREE ARCTIC GRAY WOLVES WHO PLAY AN INTEGRAL ROLE IN EDUCATING VISITORS.

ADDITIONALLY, THE CENTER HOSTS SPECIAL CHILDREN'S PROGRAMS AS WELL AS OTHER IMMERSIVE LECTURES AND SEMINARS.

BEFORE LEAVING THE CENTER, BE SURE TO CHECK OUT THE AWESOME GIFT SHOP WHERE YOU CAN PICK UP FEARSOME WOLF MERCHANDISE.

ADDRESS: 1396 MN-169, ELY, MN 55731, UNITED STATES

PASSPORT STAMPS:

NOTES :

The Frederick R. Weisman Art Museum

VISITED DATE :   SPRING ◯   SUMMER ◯   FALL ◯   WINTER ◯

WEATHER :   ☀️◯   🌤️◯   🌧️◯   🌨️◯   ⛈️◯   💨◯   🌡️TEMP :

FEE(S) :   RATING : ☆ ☆ ☆ ☆ ☆   WILL I RETURN?   YES / NO

LODGING :   WHO I WENT WITH :

DESCRIPTION / THINGS TO DO :

CULTURAL THINGS TO DO IN MINNESOTA ARE NOT HARD TO COME BY, BUT NONE ARE AS WORTHY AS THE FREDERICK R. WEISMAN ART MUSEUM.

LOCATED ON THE CAMPUS OF THE UNIVERSITY OF MINNESOTA, THIS MUSEUM WAS ESTABLISHED IN 1934 AND NAMED FOR A FAMOUS ART COLLECTOR.

SIGNIFICANTLY, THE MUSEUM AIMS TO SPARK CREATIVITY, DISCOVERY, AND CHANGE. BEING A TEACHING MUSEUM, ITS MAIN FOCUS IS EDUCATION THROUGH THE EXPERIENCE OF ART.

BEST OF ALL, THE MUSEUM IS A WELCOMING COMMUNITY ESTABLISHMENT THAT MAKES ART ACCESSIBLE TO ALL VISITORS.

WHEN VISITING THIS STUNNING MUSEUM, YOU CAN ENJOY GUIDED TOURS OF AN ARRAY OF THOUGHT-PROVOKING GALLERIES.

SOME OF THE MUSEUM'S PERMANENT EXHIBITS MAKE USE OF MEDIUMS SUCH AS CERAMICS, PAINTINGS, PHOTOGRAPHY, PRINTS, DRAWINGS, POSTERS, AND FURNITURE.

FINALLY, A VISIT TO THE MUSEUM IS ALWAYS A NEW EXPERIENCE AS THE EXHIBITS ARE EVER-CHANGING; NEW COLLECTIONS ARE ALWAYS ON THE HORIZON.

FOLLOWING YOUR IMMERSIVE TOUR OF THE MUSEUM BE SURE TO MEANDER THE BEAUTIFUL CAMPUS WHERE YOU CAN ENJOY PUBLIC ARTWORK SUCH AS ENORMOUS SCULPTURES.

ADDRESS: 333 E RIVER PKWY, MINNEAPOLIS, MN 55455, UNITED STATES

PASSPORT STAMPS:

NOTES :

The Historic Congdon Estate

VISTED DATE :   SPRING ◯ SUMMER ◯ FALL ◯ WINTER ◯

WEATHER : ☀ ◯ ⛅ ◯ 🌧 ◯ 🌨 ◯ ⛈ ◯ 🌬 ◯   🌡 TEMP :

FEE(S) :   RATING : ☆ ☆ ☆ ☆ ☆   WILL I RETURN? YES / NO

LODGING :   WHO I WENT WITH :

DESCRIPTION / THINGS TO DO :

OTHERWISE KNOWN AS GLENSHEEN MANSION, THE HISTORIC CONGDON ESTATE IS A 20,000 SQUARE FOOT MANSION SET IN DULUTH, MINNESOTA.

RUN BY THE UNIVERSITY OF MINNESOTA AS A HISTORIC PROPERTY, THE ESTATE IS ONE OF THE COOLEST PLACES TO GO IN THE STATE.

A CELEBRATION OF PRESERVATION, CONGDON ESTATE SITS ON THE GORGEOUS SHORE OF LAKE SUPERIOR AND IS A 20TH-CENTURY TESTAMENT TO DULUTH ARCHITECTURE.

OF NOTE, THE PROPERTY RESIDES ON A WHOPPING 12 ACRES OF PRISTINE LANDSCAPING ALL OF WHICH CAN BE TOURED DURING YOUR VISIT.

WITH MANY HISTORIC AND OPULENT THINGS TO SEE UNDER ONE ROOF, IT'S NO WONDER WHY VISITORS TO DULUTH ADORE THE PROPERTY.

TOUR OPTIONS INCLUDE A CLASSIC TOUR THAT IS AN ABBREVIATED TOUR OF THE FULL MANSION TOUR THAT SHOWS ALL FIVE FLOORS AND ALL OF THE ASTOUNDING 39 ROOMS.

BEYOND TOURING THE MANSION ITSELF, VISITORS ARE WELCOME TO TOUR THE GROUNDS OF THE LAKESIDE ESTATE. WITH GARDENS AND PICTURESQUE SHORELINES APLENTY, THIS GROUND TOUR IS A WONDERFUL ADD-ON TO ANY MANSION TOUR. ONE OF MANY HISTORIC MINNESOTA ATTRACTIONS, A TOUR OF THE HISTORIC CONGDON ESTATE IS ONE FOR THE AGES.

ADDRESS: 3300 LONDON RD, DULUTH, MN 55804, UNITED STATES

PASSPORT STAMPS:

NOTES :

James J. Hill House

VISTED DATE :   SPRING ◯   SUMMER ◯   FALL ◯   WINTER ◯

WEATHER :   ☀️◯   ⛅◯   🌧️◯   🌨️◯   ⛈️◯   🌬️◯   🌡️TEMP :

FEE(S) :   RATING : ☆ ☆ ☆ ☆ ☆   WILL I RETURN?   YES / NO

LODGING :   WHO I WENT WITH :

DESCRIPTION / THINGS TO DO :

IF YOU'RE WONDERING WHAT TO DO IN MINNESOTA, MAKE SURE TO CHECK OUT JAMES J. HILL HOUSE.

ESTABLISHED IN 1891 AND SITUATED ON A LOVELY TRACT IN SAINT PAUL, MINNESOTA, THE HOUSE IS A HISTORIC SIGHTSEEING DELIGHT.

THE MANSION, BUILT AND OWNED BY A RAILROAD MOGUL, SYMBOLIZES SUCCESS AND A ROMANESQUE AESTHETIC.

COSTING NEARLY ONE MILLION DOLLARS, A FORTUNE AT THE TIME, THE HOUSE EMBRACES CONSTRUCTIONS, TRENDS, AND FURNISHINGS OF THE TIME.

ASTOUNDINGLY, THE HOUSE COMPRISES 36,500 SQUARE FEET OF OPULENCE.

THE JAMES J. HILL HOUSE CONSISTS OF 13 BATHROOMS, 22 FIREPLACES, 16 CHANDELIERS, AN ART GALLERY, AN 88-FOOT RECEPTION HALL, AND MANY OTHER EXTRAVAGANT SPACES.

OTHER INTERESTING MANSION FEATURES INCLUDE CARVED OAK AND MAHOGANY WOODWORK, A THREE-STORY PIPE ORGAN, AND FUTURISTIC (AT THE TIME) MECHANISMS SUCH AS CENTRAL HEATING, ELECTRIC LIGHTING, AND SECURITY.

ONE OF MANY GORGEOUS HISTORIC PLACES TO GO IN MN, JAMES J. HILL HOUSE SHOULD FIND A SPOT ON YOUR TRAVEL PLAN.

ADDRESS: 240 SUMMIT AVE, ST PAUL, MN 55102, UNITED STATES

PASSPORT STAMPS:

NOTES :

Split Rock Lighthouse

VISTED DATE :   SPRING ◯   SUMMER ◯   FALL ◯   WINTER ◯

WEATHER :   ☀ ◯   ⛅ ◯   🌧 ◯   🌨 ◯   ⛈ ◯   🌬 ◯   🌡 TEMP :

FEE(S) :   RATING : ☆ ☆ ☆ ☆ ☆   WILL I RETURN?   YES / NO

LODGING :   WHO I WENT WITH :

DESCRIPTION / THINGS TO DO :

NESTLED ON A CLIFF OF SILVER BAY ON THE NORTH SHORE OF LAKES SUPERIOR, SPLIT ROCK LIGHTHOUSE IS QUITE POSSIBLY ONE OF THE STATE'S MOST MAGNIFICENT SIGHTSEEING DESTINATIONS.

ONE OF THE TOP TOURIST SPOTS IN ALL OF MINNESOTA, THIS LANDMARK DESERVES A PLACE IN YOUR TRAVEL PLANS.

WHETHER COMING FOR THE UNSURPASSED VIEWS OR THE LANDMARK'S INTERESTING HISTORY, YOU WON'T BE DISAPPOINTED.

VISITORS CAN PAY A NOMINAL ADMISSIONS FEE TO CLIMB THE CENTURY-OLD LIGHTHOUSE THAT SITS ATOP A GORGEOUS 130-FOOT CLIFF.

BUILT IN 1910, THIS HISTORICAL LANDMARK IS A MIGHTY 602 FEET ABOVE SEA LEVEL, TOWERS 54 FEET HIGH, AND ITS LIGHT TRAVELS A DISTANCE OF MORE THAN 20 MILES.

EACH YEAR, THE LIGHTHOUSE DRAWS VISITORS FROM AROUND THE WORLD WHO COME TO BASK IN THE STRUCTURE'S UNPARALLELED BEAUTY.

DURING A TOUR OF THE LIGHTHOUSE, VISITORS MAY ALSO ENJOY A SPECIALLY CURATED KEEPER'S TOUR THAT IMPARTS THE INS AND OUTS OF LIGHTHOUSE KEEPING.

GROUND TOURS ARE ANOTHER AWESOME WAY TO ENJOY SPLIT ROCK LIGHTHOUSE.

ADDRESS: 3713 SPLIT ROCK LIGHTHOUSE RD, TWO HARBORS, MN 55616, UNITED STATES

PASSPORT STAMPS:

NOTES :

RockFilter Distillery

VISTED DATE :   SPRING ◯   SUMMER ◯   FALL ◯   WINTER ◯

WEATHER :   ☀ ◯   ⛅ ◯   🌧 ◯   🌨 ◯   ⛈ ◯   🌬 ◯   🌡 TEMP :

FEE(S) :   RATING : ☆ ☆ ☆ ☆ ☆   WILL I RETURN?   YES / NO

LODGING :   WHO I WENT WITH :

DESCRIPTION / THINGS TO DO :

ONE OF THE LOTS OF COOL THINGS TO DO IN MINNESOTA, A TRIP TO ROCKFILTER DISTILLERY IS A UNIQUE FARM-TO-TABLE EXPERIENCE.

FOUNDED BY AN ORGANIC FARMER AND NAVY COMBAT FIGHTER PILOT, THE DISTILLERY COUPLES ONE MAN'S LOVE FOR FARMING WITH HIS AFFINITY FOR WHISKEYS AND BOURBONS.

WITH THE HARD WORK OF TOILING HIS FARM'S LAND AS WELL AS A KEEN AWARENESS AND APPRECIATION FOR LOCAL RESOURCES, ROCKFILTER DISTILLERY DISTILLS WHISKEY BY THE GALLONS USING THE SAME PRINCIPLES AS KENTUCKY BOURBONS.

AS LOCAL FARMERS AND DISTILLERS, THE ROCKFILTER DISTILLERY UTILIZES MINNESOTA'S NATURAL GEOLOGY, A HISTORIC MILL, AND THE RUSHING WATERS OF BEAVER CREEK TO PUT OUT AN EXCELLENT SPIRIT.

WHAT'S BEST, THE ROCK FILTER DISTILLERY OFFERS ONCE MONTHLY TOURS THAT INVITE VISITORS LIKE YOU TO ENJOY A UNIQUE EXPERIENCE.

DURING A TOUR, YOU CAN SEE/LEARN HOW WHISKEY IS MADE, ENJOY A TASTING, AND HANG OUT FOR A HAPPY HOUR.

ADDRESS: 113 MAPLE DR, SPRING GROVE, MN 55974, UNITED STATES

PASSPORT STAMPS:

NOTES :

Minnesota History Center

VISTED DATE :　　　　　SPRING ◯　SUMMER ◯　FALL ◯　WINTER ◯

WEATHER :　☀️◯　⛅◯　🌧️◯　🌨️◯　⛈️◯　🌬️◯　🌡️ TEMP :

FEE(S) :　　　RATING : ☆ ☆ ☆ ☆ ☆　　　WILL I RETURN?　YES / NO

LODGING :　　　　　　　WHO I WENT WITH :

DESCRIPTION / THINGS TO DO :

ANOTHER OF MANY PLACES OF INTEREST, THE MINNESOTA HISTORY CENTER IS SITUATED IN THE STATE'S CAPITAL, ONE OF MN'S FINEST BUILDINGS. SIGNIFICANTLY, THE CENTER RETELLS MINNESOTA'S RICH HIST-ORY THROUGH CAREFULLY CURATED HISTORICAL ARTIFACTS AND ARTWORK.

THE CENTER HAS LOVELY EXHIBITS, MUSICAL PERFORMANCES, CRAFTS, LECTURES, SHOPPING, AND EVEN DELICIOUS FOOD.

THE MUSEUM SECTION OF THE CENTER TAKES VISITORS ON A TOUR OF THE STATE'S AUTHENTIC HISTORY THROUGH INTERACTIVE EXPERIENCES AND HIGHLY ENTERTAINING PRESENTATIONS. IF YOU'RE LOOKING FOR AN EXPERIENCE THAT COUPLES ENTERTAINMENT WITH UNIQUE THINGS TO SEE, THIS IS THE PLACE FOR YOU. FURTHERMORE, THE CENTER HAS MANY WONDERFUL AND WELCOMING COMMUNITY SPACES.

FOR INSTANCE, A SUSPENDED AIRPLANE IN THE MAIN ROTUNDA, A GIANT MINNESOTA POSTCARD THAT SERVES AS AN AWESOME PHOTO BACKDROP, AND THE ROTUNDA'S UNIQUE CHARM BRACELET EMBEDDED IN THE FLOOR ARE ALL REMARKABLE FEATURES OF THE CENTER.

ANOTHER AWESOME CENTER FEATURE IS THE BREATHTAKING VIEW OF THE CAPITOL SEEN THROUGH THE PICTURE WINDOW OF THE GREAT HALL.

ONE OF THE MOST INTERESTING PLACES TO VISIT IN THE GOPHER STATE, BE SURE TO MAKE TIME FOR THE MINNESOTA HISTORY CENTER.

ADDRESS: 345 W KELLOGG BLVD, ST PAUL, MN 55102, UNITED STATES

PASSPORT STAMPS:

NOTES :

Lake Superior Marine Museum

VISTED DATE :   SPRING ◯   SUMMER ◯   FALL ◯   WINTER ◯

WEATHER :   ☀️◯   ⛅◯   🌧️◯   🌨️◯   ⛈️◯   🌬️◯   🌡️TEMP :

FEE(S) :   RATING : ☆ ☆ ☆ ☆ ☆   WILL I RETURN?   YES / NO

LODGING :   WHO I WENT WITH :

DESCRIPTION / THINGS TO DO :

RESIDING IN DULUTH, MINNESOTA, THE LAKE SUPERIOR MARINE MUSEUM IS ONE OF THE STATE'S MANY NOTABLE POINTS OF INTEREST. RUN BY THE UNITED STATES ARMY CORPS OF ENGINEERS, THIS MUSEUM OVERLOOKS THE DULUTH-SUPERIOR HARBOR.

WITH THE LAUDABLE AIM OF PRESERVING LAKE SUPERIOR'S MARITIME HERITAGE, THE MUSEUM PRESERVES AND EXHIBITS MARITIME ARTIFACTS, DOCUMENTS, AND MORE.

ADDITIONALLY, THE MUSEUM HAS A VAST COLLECTION OF PHOTOGRAPHS, PUBLICATIONS, AND EDUCATIONAL MATERIALS.

IF YOU'RE LOOKING FOR COOL STUFF TO DO WITH A PENCHANT FOR HISTORY, THE LAKE SUPERIOR MARINE MUSEUM IS A GREAT PLACE TO CHECK OUT.

OPENED THURSDAY THROUGH SUNDAY, ADMISSION TO THE MUSEUM IS FREE.

DURING YOUR VISIT, YOU'LL ENJOY A JOURNEY THROUGH THE HISTORY OF THE GREAT LAKES.

SOME OF THE EXCITING EXHIBITS SHOWCASE SHIPWRECKS, GREAT LAKES VESSELS, GREAT LAKES INDUSTRIAL HISTORY, AND BEYOND.

A PERFECT PLACE FOR THE WHOLE FAMILY TO ENJOY AND LEARN FROM, THE LAKE SUPERIOR MARINE MUSEUM IS ONE OF MANY COOL THINGS TO DO IN THE GOPHER STATE.

ADDRESS: 600 CANAL PARK DR, DULUTH, MN 55802, UNITED STATES

PASSPORT STAMPS:

NOTES :

Minneapolis Sculpture Garden

VISTED DATE :   SPRING ◯   SUMMER ◯   FALL ◯   WINTER ◯

WEATHER :   ☀️◯   ⛅◯   🌧️◯   🌨️◯   ⛈️◯   🌬️◯   🌡️TEMP :

FEE(S) :   RATING : ☆ ☆ ☆ ☆ ☆   WILL I RETURN?   YES / NO

LODGING :   WHO I WENT WITH :

DESCRIPTION / THINGS TO DO :

QUITE POSSIBLY, ONE OF THE MOST BEAUTIFUL PLACES IN THE UNITED STATES, THE MINNEAPOLIS SCULPTURE GARDEN IS SITUATED ON 11 ACRES OF A PUBLIC PARK IN MINNESOTA.

IF YOU'RE LOOKING FOR THINGS TO DO IN MN THAT WILL GET YOU OUTDOORS AND ENJOYING NATURE, THIS IS THE SPOT TO DO IT.

THIS FREE ATTRACTION IS ONE THE WHOLE FAMILY CAN ENJOY.

OPEN 365 DAYS A YEAR FROM DAWN TO MIDNIGHT, ANYTIME, TODAY, TOMORROW, OR THIS WEEKEND IS A GOOD TIME TO VISIT.

WHILE WALKING THE GROUNDS OF THE GARDEN, VISITORS ARE TREATED TO ASTOUNDING SCULPTURES BY TWIN CITY ARTISTS.

HOUSING A REMARKABLE COLLECTION OF MODERN AND CONTEMPORARY ARTWORK, THE GARDEN ALLOWS VISITORS TO COME FACE TO FACE WITH AND INTERACT WITH THE ARTWORK, AN EXPERIENCE A TRADITIONAL MUSEUM DOESN'T TYPICALLY PERMIT.

BEST OF ALL, THE METICULOUSLY LANDSCAPED SETTING ADDS A SECONDARY ELEMENT THAT MAKES THE GARDEN ONE OF THE BEST PLACES TO VISIT IN MINNESOTA.

ADDRESS: 725 VINELAND PL, MINNEAPOLIS, MN 55403, UNITED STATES

PASSPORT STAMPS:

NOTES :

North American Bear Center

VISITED DATE :　　　　　SPRING ◯　SUMMER ◯　FALL ◯　WINTER ◯

WEATHER :　☀ ◯　⛅ ◯　🌧 ◯　🌨 ◯　⛈ ◯　🌬 ◯　🌡 TEMP :

FEE(S) :　　　RATING : ☆ ☆ ☆ ☆ ☆　　WILL I RETURN?　YES / NO

LODGING :　　　　　　　WHO I WENT WITH :

DESCRIPTION / THINGS TO DO :

THE NORTH AMERICAN BEAR CENTER IS ONE OF MANY UNIQUE PLACES TO VISIT IN MN.

LOCATED IN ELY, MINNESOTA, THIS ESTABLISHMENT IS HOUSED NEAR THE PINE FOREST AND EDUCATES VISITORS ABOUT REGIONAL BLACK BEARS AND OTHER WILDLIFE.

ONE OF THE ONLY CENTERS OF ITS KIND, THE CENTER TEACHES VISITORS ABOUT BEAR BEHAVIOR, HABITATS, ECOLOGY, AND HOW THEY RELATE TO HUMANS.

WITHIN THE CENTER ARE AMAZING ARTIFACTS SUCH AS UNIQUE BEAR DISPLAYS, POSTERS, AND PHOTOGRAPHS.

WORKING CLOSELY WITH THE LOCAL WILDLIFE REFUGE, THE CENTER EMPLOYS RENOWNED BIOLOGISTS WHO ARE EXPERTS ON THE TOPIC OF BEARS.

THE EXPERTISE OF THESE SCIENTISTS COUPLED WITH THE VISUAL ARTIFACTS MAKES FOR A UNIQUE AND IMMERSIVE EXPERIENCE.

ASTONISHINGLY, THE CENTER FEATURES BEAR MOUNTS THAT EXEMPLIFY BLACK BEARS, POLAR BEARS, AND GRIZZLY BEARS, ALL POSED WITH EXCEPTIONAL REALISM.

LASTLY, THE CENTER ALSO HOSTS SPECIAL PROGRAMMING SUCH AS BEHIND-THE-SCENES TOURS, A BROADCAST PROGRAM, AND A DINNER-TIME PROGRAM.

ADDRESS: 1926 MN-169, ELY, MN 55731, UNITED STATES

PASSPORT STAMPS:

NOTES :

Science Museum of Minnesota

VISTED DATE :   SPRING ◯ SUMMER ◯ FALL ◯ WINTER ◯

WEATHER : ☀ ◯ ⛅ ◯ 🌧 ◯ 🌨 ◯ ⛈ ◯ 🌬 ◯   TEMP :

FEE(S) :   RATING : ☆ ☆ ☆ ☆ ☆   WILL I RETURN? YES / NO

LODGING :   WHO I WENT WITH :

DESCRIPTION / THINGS TO DO :

THE SCIENCE MUSEUM OF MINNESOTA IS ONE OF THE GOPHER STATE'S POINTS OF INTEREST THAT ANSWERS THE PRESSING QUESTION OF WHAT TO DO WHEN VISITING THE STATE.

THE MUSEUM, FOUNDED IN 1907 AND SITUATED IN THE HEART OF SAINT PAUL, FOCUSES ON SCIENTIFIC TOPICS OF TECHNOLOGY, MATHEMATICS, PHYSICAL SCIENCE, AND THE NATURAL SCIENCES.

WITH SO MUCH TO LEARN AND SEE UNDER ONE ROOF, IT'S NO SURPRISE THAT TRAVELERS COME FROM FAR AND WIDE TO ENJOY ONE OF THE BEST MINNESOTA ATTRACTIONS.

WITH NEARLY NINE ACRES OF EXHIBITS AND PROGRAMMING, THE MUSEUM PROVIDES VISITORS WITH ENDLESS OPPORTUNITIES TO LEARN, EXPLORE, AND EXPERIENCE.

OF NOTE, THE MUSEUM IS HOME TO PALEONTOLOGICAL EXHIBITS, AN EXPERIMENT GALLERY, FOSSIL EXHIBITS, A HUMAN BODY GALLERY, A RACE EXHIBIT, AND A MISSISSIPPI RIVER GALLERY; THERE IS SO MUCH TO ENCOUNTER AT THIS WORLD-CLASS MUSEUM.

IF YOU'RE WONDERING WHERE TO GO WHEN VISITING MN, WONDER NO MORE!

ADDRESS: 120 W KELLOGG BLVD, ST PAUL, MN 55102, UNITED STATES

PASSPORT STAMPS:

NOTES :

Mill City Museum

VISTED DATE : SPRING ◯ SUMMER ◯ FALL ◯ WINTER ◯

WEATHER : ☀ ◯ 🌤 ◯ 🌧 ◯ 🌨 ◯ ⛈ ◯ 🌬 ◯ 🌡 TEMP :

FEE(S) : RATING : ☆ ☆ ☆ ☆ ☆ WILL I RETURN? YES / NO

LODGING : WHO I WENT WITH :

DESCRIPTION / THINGS TO DO :

THE MILL CITY MUSEUM, WHICH IS OPERATED BY THE MINNESOTA HISTORICAL SOCIETY, IS HOUSED IN THE RUINS OF THE WASHBURN MILL ADJACENT TO THE MISSISSIPPI RIVER.

THE MUSEUM ITSELF IS AN ARCHITECTURAL WONDER THAT IN AND OF ITSELF WARRANTS A TRIP TO THIS MOST UNIQUE OF MINNESOTA ATTRACTIONS. NOTABLY, THE BUILDING IS EIGHT STORIES TALL WITHIN AN OLD LIMESTONE MILL. NESTLED ON THE BEAUTIFUL RIVERBANK, THE MUSEUM HOUSES UNIQUE ARTIFACTS OF LOCAL AND MILLING HISTORY.

SIGNIFICANTLY, THE MILL CITY MUSEUM IS HOME TO OLD MILLING EQUIPMENT, VINTAGE PROPAGANDA, WHEAT FARM ARTIFACTS, AND MORE.

ONE OF THE MUSEUM'S FLOORS IS HOME TO THE FORMER PACKING FLOOR AND IT SHOWCASES ROTATING SPECIAL EXHIBITS.

ESSENTIALLY, YOUR EXPERIENCE AT THE MUSEUM IS HEIGHTENED BY A MARRIAGE OF RAW POWER, ASTOUNDING VIEWS, AND INTERACTIVE EXHIBITS.

SOME NOTEWORTHY EXHIBITS INCLUDE THE FLOUR TOWER, THE BAKING LAB, THE WATER LAB, AND MORE.

ONE OF THE BEST, MOST ENJOYABLE PLACES TO GO IN MINNESOTA, MAKE SURE TO ADD MILL CITY MUSEUM TO YOUR TRAVEL PLANS.

ADDRESS: 704 S 2ND ST, MINNEAPOLIS, MN 55401, UNITED STATES

PASSPORT STAMPS:

NOTES :

7 Vines Vineyard

VISTED DATE :　　　　　　SPRING ◯　SUMMER ◯　FALL ◯　WINTER ◯

WEATHER :　☀◯　⛅◯　🌧◯　🌨◯　⛈◯　🌬◯　🌡 TEMP :

FEE(S) :　　　　RATING : ☆ ☆ ☆ ☆ ☆　　WILL I RETURN?　YES / NO

LODGING :　　　　　　　　WHO I WENT WITH :

DESCRIPTION / THINGS TO DO :

SITUATED ON A GORGEOUS FARM IN DELLWOOD, MINNESOTA, 7 VINES VINEYARD IS THE SUCCESSFUL PASSION PROJECT OF SAINT PAUL HIGH SCHOOL SWEETHEARTS.

ESTABLISHED IN 2010 IN AN IDYLLIC SETTING, THE VINEYARD IS ONE OF THE TOP PLACES TO VISIT IN MN.

ESSENTIALLY, FROM THE COUPLE'S ADORATION FOR THE FARM ALONG WITH THEIR LOVE OF WINE SPRANG 7 VINES VINEYARD.

WITH THE PLANTING OF THEIR FIRST PLANTS AND THE ERECTION OF THE WINERY BUILDING IN 2012, MINNESOTA WELCOMED ITS BEST WINERY IN THE STATE.

DURING A VISIT TO THE WINERY, GUESTS CAN ENJOY PRIVATE AND PUBLIC TOURS, WINE TASTINGS, AND DELICIOUS PAIRINGS IN THE RENOWNED RESTAURANT.

TOURS INCLUDE AN OVERVIEW OF THE WINERY AS WELL AS THE HISTORIC TRACT IT SITS UPON.

IN ADDITION TO STANDARD FARE WINERY ACTIVITIES, 7 VINES VINEYARD ALSO HOSTS WEEKLY YOGA ON THE PROPERTY.

IF YOU'RE IN THE MARKET FOR SOME GROWN-UP FUN WHEN VISITING MN TODAY OR THIS WEEKEND, BE SURE TO PLAN A VISIT TO 7 VINES VINEYARD.

ADDRESS: 101 MN-96, DELLWOOD, MN 55110, UNITED STATES

PASSPORT STAMPS:

NOTES :

National Eagle Center

VISTED DATE :　　　　　　　SPRING ◯　SUMMER ◯　FALL ◯　WINTER ◯

WEATHER :　☀ ◯　⛅ ◯　🌧 ◯　🌨 ◯　⛈ ◯　🌬 ◯　　🌡 TEMP :

FEE(S) :　　　　RATING : ☆ ☆ ☆ ☆ ☆　　　WILL I RETURN?　YES / NO

LODGING :　　　　　　　　WHO I WENT WITH :

DESCRIPTION / THINGS TO DO :

THE NATIONAL EAGLE CENTER IN WABASHA, MINNESOTA WORKS TIRELESSLY TO EDUCATE VISITORS ABOUT THE ECOLOGY, BIOLOGY, AND NATURAL HISTORY OF EAGLES.

ONE OF THE MOST STUNNING POINTS OF INTEREST IN THE AREA, THE NATIONAL EAGLE CENTER CONNECTS VISITORS TO THIS MAJESTIC AVIARY CREATURE AS WELL AS ITS HISTORICAL SYMBOLISM IN THE UNITED STATES.

WITH THE HOPE AND MISSION OF TEACHING WILDLIFE CONSERVATION, ESPECIALLY CONCERNING EAGLES, THE CENTER IS SITUATED IN THE MISSISSIPPI RIVER VALLEY WHICH IS HOME TO HUNDREDS OF BALD EAGLES.

ONE OF THE BEST WAYS TO EXPERIENCE ALL THE CENTER HAS TO OFFER IS THROUGH THEIR UNIQUE HABITAT TOURS.

DURING THESE TOURS, YOU CAN CATCH LIVE GLIMPSES OF BOTH BALD AND GOLDEN EAGLES IN THEIR NATURAL HABITAT.

DURING ONE OF THESE FUN TOURS, YOU'LL BE GUIDED BY THE EXPERTISE OF AN EXPERIENCED GUIDE WHO HAS SCOUTED A LOCALE IN ADVANCE.

FINALLY, A VISIT TO THE NATIONAL EAGLE CENTER BRINGS YOU AS CLOSE AS CAN BE WITH THESE STUNNING CREATURES IN ONE OF MINNESOTA'S MOST BEAUTIFUL POINTS OF INTEREST.

ADDRESS: 50 PEMBROKE AVE, WABASHA, MN 55981, UNITED STATES

PASSPORT STAMPS:

NOTES:

Minnesota Landscape Arboretum

VISTED DATE : _____ SPRING ◯ SUMMER ◯ FALL ◯ WINTER ◯

WEATHER : ☀ ◯ ⛅ ◯ ☁ ◯ 🌨 ◯ ⛈ ◯ 🌬 ◯   🌡 TEMP : _____

FEE(S) : _____ RATING : ☆ ☆ ☆ ☆ ☆   WILL I RETURN? YES / NO

LODGING : _____   WHO I WENT WITH : _____

DESCRIPTION / THINGS TO DO :

THIS 1,200-ACRE HORTICULTURAL ATTRACTION IS ONE OF THE MOST BEAUTIFUL SITES TO VISIT IN ALL OF MINNESOTA.

LOCATED IN CHASKA, MN, ONLY FOUR MILES OUTSIDE OF CHANHASSEN, THE ARBORETUM BRINGS VISITORS FACE TO FACE WITH SOME OF THE MOST GORGEOUS LANDSCAPES IN THE GOPHER STATE.

WITH EVER-CHANGING SEASONAL DISPLAYS, SITUATED BOTH INDOORS AND OUTDOORS, THE MINNESOTA LANDSCAPE ARBORETUM IS A TOP ATTRACTION.

OF NOTE, THE ARBORETUM'S MISSION IS TO EDUCATE, INFORM, AND SHARE WITH VISITORS ABOUT HORTICULTURAL RESEARCH AND PROTECTED NATURAL AREAS.

SIGNIFICANTLY, THE MINNESOTA LANDSCAPE ARBORETUM IS HOME TO 21 MODEL LANDSCAPES, 28 GARDENS, 44 COLLECTIONS, AND 216 WORKS OF ART.

DURING A TOUR OF THIS FAMILY-FRIENDLY FACILITY, VISITORS CAN ENJOY ANYTHING FROM HERB AND PERENNIAL GARDENS TO DEMONSTRATION GARDENS AND RAIN GARDENS.

THE BREADTH OF NATURAL SCENERY ON DISPLAY AT THE ARBORETUM IS UNPRECEDENTED, MAKING IT ONE OF MANY TOP PLACES TO VISIT IN MINNESOTA.

ADDRESS: 3675 ARBORETUM DR, CHASKA, MN 55318, UNITED STATES

PASSPORT STAMPS:

NOTES :

Leif Erickson Park and Rose Garden

VISTED DATE :   SPRING ◯ SUMMER ◯ FALL ◯ WINTER ◯

WEATHER :   ☀ ◯   ⛅ ◯   🌧 ◯   ❄ ◯   ⛈ ◯   💨 ◯   🌡TEMP :

FEE(S) :   RATING : ☆ ☆ ☆ ☆ ☆   WILL I RETURN?   YES / NO

LODGING :   WHO I WENT WITH :

DESCRIPTION / THINGS TO DO :

LOCATED IN DULUTH, A SUBURB OF NORTHEAST MINNESOTA, LEIF ERICKSON PARK & ROSE GARDEN IS A BEAUTIFUL LOCALE ALONG THE SHORES OF LAKE SUPERIOR.

WITH SO MANY THINGS TO DO IN MN, IT'S EASY TO OVERLOOK THE STATE'S PARK SYSTEMS.

HOWEVER, LEIF ERICKSON PARK & ROSE GARDEN PROVIDES LOVELY OPPORTUNITIES FOR HIKING, RECREATION, AND SIGHTSEEING.

A DELIGHTFUL PICNIC ON THE BEACH OR A BALL GAME IN ONE OF THE PARK'S OPEN FIELDS ARE JUST A FEW OF THE WAYS TO ENJOY THIS PARK.

WITHIN THE LEIF ERICKSON PARK SITS THE ROSE GARDEN WHICH WAS ESTABLISHED IN 1965 AND IS HOME TO MORE THAN 2,000 ROSES.

PERFECTLY CURATED AND ARRANGED IN CURVING AND CASCADING BEDS, SOME OF WHICH SURROUND A CENTRAL FOUNTAIN, THE ROSE GARDEN IS A SIGHT TO BEHOLD.

ADDITIONALLY, THE GARDEN FEATURES A STUNNING GAZEBO THAT IS ALSO SURROUNDED BY LABELED ROSES; THE GAZEBO CAN BE ACCESSED BY INTERWOVEN PATHWAYS THAT ARE ALSO BEAUTIFULLY LANDSCAPED.

ADDRESS: 1301 LONDON RD, DULUTH, MN 55805, UNITED STATES

PASSPORT STAMPS:

NOTES :

Minnehaha Park

VISTED DATE : SPRING ◯ SUMMER ◯ FALL ◯ WINTER ◯

WEATHER : ☀ ◯ ⛅ ◯ 🌧 ◯ 🌨 ◯ ⛈ ◯ 🌬 ◯   🌡 TEMP :

FEE(S) : RATING : ☆ ☆ ☆ ☆ ☆   WILL I RETURN? YES / NO

LODGING : WHO I WENT WITH :

DESCRIPTION / THINGS TO DO :

ONE OF THE LOVELIEST TOURIST ATTRACTIONS IN MINNESOTA, MINNEHAHA PARK IS A CITY PARK IN MINNEAPOLIS. THE PARK PROVIDES THE PERFECT LANDSCAPE FOR LOADS OF OUTDOOR FUN.

WITH BOTH DEVELOPED AND UNDEVELOPED AREAS OF THE PARK, YOU CAN ENJOY THE LANDSCAPE HOWEVER BEST SUITS YOU.

FOR INSTANCE, SOME OF THE PARK'S FEATURES AND AMENITIES INCLUDE A BANDSTAND, A BIKING PATH, A PICNIC AREA, A PLAYGROUND, PUBLIC ART, A VOLLEYBALL COURT, A WADING POOL, AND A WALKING PATH. WITH ALL OF THESE FABULOUS PARK FEATURES, YOU'LL NEVER WONDER WHAT TO DO AT MINNEHAHA PARK.

ADDITIONALLY, MINNEHAHA PARK HAS THREE BEAUTIFUL GARDENS AND THREE HISTORICAL SITES, ALL OF WHICH CAN BE TOURED AT YOUR LEISURE.

MOREOVER, THE PARK IS ALSO HOME TO A DOG PARK, HIKING TRAILS, AND EVEN A RESTAURANT.

LASTLY, THE PARK OFTEN HOSTS CULTURAL EVENTS LIKE LIVE MUSIC AND MOVIES IN THE PARK.

WITH OVER 165 ACRES TO EXPLORE, IT'S NO WONDER VISITORS COME FROM FAR AND WIDE TO ENJOY MINNEHAHA PARK.

ADDRESS: 4801 MINNEHAHA AVE, MINNEAPOLIS, MN 55417, UNITED STATES

PASSPORT STAMPS:

NOTES :

Quarry Hill Nature Center

VISTED DATE :   SPRING ◯   SUMMER ◯   FALL ◯   WINTER ◯

WEATHER :   ☀◯   ⛅◯   ☁◯   🌨◯   ⛈◯   🌬◯   🌡TEMP :

FEE(S) :   RATING :   ☆ ☆ ☆ ☆ ☆   WILL I RETURN?   YES / NO

LODGING :   WHO I WENT WITH :

DESCRIPTION / THINGS TO DO :

LOCATED IN THE HEART OF ROCHESTER, MINNESOTA, QUARRY HILL NATURE CENTER OPENED ITS DOORS IN 1972. SINCE THAT TIME, THE CENTER HAS BEEN REDEFINED, IMPROVED UPON, AND EXPANDED.

TODAY, QUARRY HILL NATURE CENTER IS A PREMIER DESTINATION FOR THOSE INTERESTED IN ENVIRONMENTAL AFFAIRS.

FULL OF HISTORY-RICH LOCALES, THE CENTER IS ONE OF A FEW PLACES TO GO LIKE IT IN MINNESOTA.

SITUATED AMID A BEAUTIFUL PARK SETTING, THE CENTER IS HOME TO LOVELY HIKING TRAILS, BIRD WATCHING, AND FOSSIL HUNTING.

WITHIN THE NATURE CENTER, VISITORS ARE WELCOME TO MEET MORE THAN 30 VARIETIES OF LIVE ANIMALS SUCH AS BIRDS AND FISH AS WELL AS AN EXTENSIVE TAXIDERMY COLLECTION.

ADDITIONALLY, THE CENTER'S OBSERVABLE HONEYBEE HIVES ARE SUPER INTRIGUING TO WATCH UP CLOSE.

SURROUNDED BY MORE THAN 300 ACRES OF PARK, QUARRY HILL NATURE CENTER IS A BEAUTIFUL PLACE TO EXPLORE AND LEARN ABOUT A VARIETY OF ANIMALS, ECOSYSTEMS, AND GEOLOGICAL FORMATIONS.

ADDRESS: 701 SILVER CREEK RD NE, ROCHESTER, MN 55906, UNITED STATES

PASSPORT STAMPS:

NOTES :

Superior National Forest

VISTED DATE :   SPRING ◯   SUMMER ◯   FALL ◯   WINTER ◯

WEATHER : ☀ ◯   ⛅ ◯   🌧 ◯   🌨 ◯   ⛈ ◯   🌬 ◯   🌡 TEMP :

FEE(S) :   RATING : ☆ ☆ ☆ ☆ ☆   WILL I RETURN?   YES / NO

LODGING :   WHO I WENT WITH :

DESCRIPTION / THINGS TO DO :

SITUATED IN ARROWHEAD, MINNESOTA, RIGHT BETWEEN CANADA AND THE US, SITS THIS AMAZING FOREST SYSTEM.

FOUNDED IN 1909, SUPERIOR NATIONAL FOREST IS KNOWN FOR ITS DIVERSE ECOSYSTEM, A HANDFUL OF LAKES, AND ASTOUNDING HISTORY. THE ONE-MILLION-ACRE FOREST IS HOME TO A DIVERGENT COMMUNITY OF PLANTS AND ANIMALS.

WITHIN THE FOREST LIMITS ARE THE WIDE BREADTH OF NATURALLY OCCURRING SPECIMENS THAT MEET THE NEEDS OF HUMANS.

WHETHER COMING TO EXPLORE OR FORAGE, SUPERIOR NATIONAL FOREST IS ONE OF THE MOST BEAUTIFUL AND PRODUCTIVE THINGS TO DO IN MN.

IF YOU'RE LOOKING FOR MINNESOTA ATTRACTIONS THAT WILL TAKE YOU OUTDOORS FOR FUN AND OBSERVANCE OF NATURE CHECK OUT THIS PARK.

OF NOTE, POPULAR ACTIVITIES AT SUPERIOR NATIONAL FOREST INCLUDE CAMPING, FISHING, CANOEING, AND HIKING. ADDITIONALLY, THE PARK IS A PERFECT SETTING FOR CROSS COUNTRY SKIING, ICE FISHING, SWIMMING, SNOWMOBILING, AND HUNTING.

NOT ONLY CAN THE PARK BE ACCESSED BY MANY INCOMING ROADWAYS, BUT THREE SCENIC BYWAYS MAKE THE JOURNEY INTO THE PARK JUST AS INVITING AS THE PARK ITSELF.

ADDRESS: 8901 GRAND AVE PL, DULUTH, MN 55808, UNITED STATES

PASSPORT STAMPS:

NOTES :

Voyageurs National Park

VISTED DATE :   SPRING ◯   SUMMER ◯   FALL ◯   WINTER ◯

WEATHER :   ☀ ◯   ⛅ ◯   🌧 ◯   🌨 ◯   ⛈ ◯   🌬 ◯   🌡 TEMP :

FEE(S) :   RATING : ☆ ☆ ☆ ☆ ☆   WILL I RETURN?   YES / NO

LODGING :   WHO I WENT WITH :

DESCRIPTION / THINGS TO DO :

VOYAGEURS NATIONAL PARK IS ONE OF A FEW PICTURESQUE MINNESOTA ATTRACTIONS WHERE VISITORS CAN ENJOY WATER RECREATION ALL YEAR LONG.

SITUATED IN NORTHERN MINNESOTA, JUST OUTSIDE CANADA, THE PARK IS KNOWN FOR ITS FORESTRY AND THREE BEAUTIFUL LAKES.

ADDITIONALLY, THE PARK IS HOME TO THE ELLSWORTH ROCK GARDENS WHICH FEATURES SEVERAL AMAZING ABSTRACT SCULPTURES.

ADDITIONALLY, THE PARK IS HOME TO KETTLE FALLS AND AN ASTOUNDING DAM.

OF ALL THESE AWESOME ATTRACTIONS, THOUGH, NONE IS AS POPULAR AS THE LAKES THAT ARE USED BY VISITORS FOR WATERSPORTS.

SITUATED AMID OVER 200,000 ACRES OF FORESTRY ARE THE RAINY, KABETOGAMA, AND NAMAKAN LAKES.

THESE LAKES PROVIDE VISITORS THE OPPORTUNITY TO EXPLORE UNIQUE ECOSYSTEMS, ROCK RIDGES, CLIFFS, AND MORE. THE LAKES ARE ALL SUITABLE FOR SWIMMING, CANOEING, KAYAKING, AND BEYOND.

FINALLY, DEPENDING ON THE TIME OF YEAR DURING WHICH YOU VISIT, THE NORTHERN LIGHTS CAN SOMETIMES BE SEEN FROM VOYAGEURS NATIONAL PARK.

ADDRESS: INTERNATIONAL FALLS, MN 56649, UNITED STATES

PASSPORT STAMPS:

NOTES :

Mall of America

VISTED DATE :　　　　　SPRING ○　SUMMER ○　FALL ○　WINTER ○

WEATHER :　　☀ ○　🌥 ○　🌧 ○　🌨 ○　⛈ ○　🌬 ○　　🌡 TEMP :

FEE(S) :　　　RATING : ☆ ☆ ☆ ☆ ☆　　　WILL I RETURN?　YES / NO

LODGING :　　　　　　　WHO I WENT WITH :

DESCRIPTION / THINGS TO DO :

ONE OF THE MOST FAMOUS PLACES TO GO IN ALL OF MINNESOTA IS THE MALL OF AMERICA.

LOCATED ADJACENT TO MINNEAPOLIS AND NEAR THE MINNESOTA RIVER, MALL OF AMERICA OPENED ITS DOORS IN 1992 AND HAS BEEN A LEADER IN RETAIL EVER SINCE.

OF NOTE, THE MALL HAS NEARLY 40 MILLION VISITORS WALK THROUGH ITS DOORS EACH YEAR.

ADDITIONALLY, THE MALL HOSTS MORE THAN 400 SPECIAL EVENTS EVERY YEAR, EVENTS LIKE CONCERTS AND OTHER LIVE SHOWS.

WHETHER YOU'RE LOOKING TO WALK THE HALLS OF HISTORY, ENJOY SHOPPING AT ITS FINEST, OR TAKE IN A SHOW, MALL OF AMERICA IS AN AMERICAN INSTITUTION THAT HAS TO BE SEEN TO BE BELIEVED.

IN ADDITION TO THE SHOPPING AND SHOWS, THE MALL ALSO HAS MANY WORLD-RENOWNED RESTAURANTS, A THEATRE, THE CRAYOLA EXPERIENCE, AN AQUARIUM, AND LOADS MORE.

WITH SO MUCH TO DO IN ONE CENTRAL LOCATION, YOU COULD EASILY VISIT THE MALL A FEW DAYS IN A ROW AND STILL NOT SEE EVERYTHING.

ADDRESS: 60 E BROADWAY, BLOOMINGTON, MN 55425, UNITED STATES

PASSPORT STAMPS:

NOTES :

Munsinger / Clemens Gardens

VISTED DATE :   SPRING ◯   SUMMER ◯   FALL ◯   WINTER ◯

WEATHER :   ☀◯ ⛅◯ 🌧◯ 🌨◯ ⛈◯ 💨◯   🌡TEMP :

FEE(S) :   RATING : ☆ ☆ ☆ ☆ ☆   WILL I RETURN?   YES / NO

LODGING :   WHO I WENT WITH :

DESCRIPTION / THINGS TO DO :

MUNSINGER / CLEMENS GARDENS IS ACTUALLY TWO ADJACENT GARDENS SITUATED ON THE BANKS OF THE MISSISSIPPI RIVER.

ONE OF MANY BEAUTIFUL PLACES TO VISIT IN MN, THE GARDENS ARE LINED WITH RAMBLING PATHS AND PAVED WALKWAYS THAT VISITORS COME FROM FAR AND WIDE TO STROLL.

WHETHER LOOKING FOR A PLACE TO HAVE A STROLL OR PERHAPS INTERESTED IN A MUSE FOR ARTWORK AND PHOTOGRAPHY, ANYTIME IS A GOOD TIME TO VISIT THESE MINNESOTA GARDENS.

DURING SPRING, SUMMER, AND FALL, VISITORS CAN BASK IN THE UNPRECEDENTED BEAUTY OF GORGEOUSLY CURATED AND LANDSCAPED GARDENS.

THE GARDENS ARE HOME TO HUNDREDS OF VARIETIES OF ANNUALS, PERENNIALS, ORNAMENTAL GRASSES, SEASONAL FOLIAGE, AND SO MUCH MORE.

THE SPECTACULAR GARDENS OFTEN HOST SPECIAL EVENTS LIKE LIVE CONCERTS, ART FAIRS, AND PHOTOGRAPHY CONTESTS.

OPEN TO THE PUBLIC YEAR-ROUND AT NO COST, A VISIT TO MUNSINGER / CLEMENS GARDENS IS A MUST-DO.

ADDRESS: 1515 RIVERSIDE DR SE, ST CLOUD, MN 56304, UNITED STATES

PASSPORT STAMPS:

NOTES :

The Aerial Lift Bridge

VISTED DATE :   SPRING ◯   SUMMER ◯   FALL ◯   WINTER ◯

WEATHER :   ☀️◯ 🌤️◯ 🌧️◯ 🌨️◯ ⛈️◯ 🌬️◯   🌡️ TEMP :

FEE(S) :   RATING : ☆ ☆ ☆ ☆ ☆   WILL I RETURN?   YES / NO

LODGING :   WHO I WENT WITH :

DESCRIPTION / THINGS TO DO :

THE AERIAL LIFT BRIDGE IS A LANDMARK ATTRACTION IN DULUTH, MINNESOTA.

OPENING IN 1905, THE BRIDGE WAS ONE OF THE US'S FIRST TRANSPORTER BRIDGES.

IN FACT, ONLY ONE OTHER OF ITS KIND EXISTS IN THE WORLD.

WITH A 138-FOOT CLEARANCE, A TOTAL LENGTH OF 501 FEET, AND A REMARKABLE HEIGHT OF 226 FEET, THE BRIDGE IS A MARVEL TO SEE.

ESSENTIALLY, THE BRIDGE LIES LOW TO THE WATER AND IS LIFTED TO ITS MAXIMUM HEIGHT WHEN SHIPS REQUIRE PASSAGE.

AN UNUSUAL OPERATION FOR A TRANSPORTER BRIDGE, THE AERIAL LIFT BRIDGE IS A SIGHT TO BE SEEN.

REMARKABLY, THE BRIDGE CAN BE LIFTED TO ITS FULL HEIGHT IN ONLY ONE MINUTE; IT'S LIFTED NEARLY 5,000 TIMES PER YEAR.

ALTHOUGH MOST VISITORS TO THE BRIDGE MARVEL AT ITS UNIQUENESS AND THE PASSING SHIPS FROM ITS BASE, WHAT MOST DON'T KNOW IS THAT YOU CAN ACTUALLY WALK ACROSS THE BRIDGE.

IN FACT, A WALK ACROSS THE BRIDGE WILL DELIVER YOU TO OR FROM CANAL PARK, ANOTHER LOVELY MINNESOTA ATTRACTION.

ADDRESS: 601 S LAKE AVE, DULUTH, MN 55802, UNITED STATES

PASSPORT STAMPS:

NOTES :

Itasca State Park

VISTED DATE :   SPRING ◯ SUMMER ◯ FALL ◯ WINTER ◯

WEATHER : ☀◯ ⛅◯ 🌧◯ 🌨◯ ⛈◯ 🌬◯   🌡 TEMP :

FEE(S) :   RATING : ☆ ☆ ☆ ☆ ☆   WILL I RETURN? YES / NO

LODGING :   WHO I WENT WITH :

DESCRIPTION / THINGS TO DO :

HOME TO MANY TRIBUTARY STREAMS LEADING IN AND OUT OF THE MISSISSIPPI RIVER, ITASCA STATE PARK IS A GREAT PLACE TO VISIT IN MINNESOTA.

SPANNING MORE THAN 30,000 ACRES, THE PARK IS A LOVELY PLACE TO EXPLORE NATURE AND ENJOY WHOLESOME FAMILY FUN.

FIRST ESTABLISHED IN THE LATE 1800S, THE PARK IS ONE OF THE STATE'S OLDEST PARKS.

OF NOTE, THERE ARE MORE THAN A WHOPPING 100 LAKES WITHIN THE PARK BUT ITS GREATEST CLAIM ARE THE HEADWATERS CONNECTED TO THE MISSISSIPPI RIVER.

WITH SO MANY THINGS TO DO IN MINNESOTA, YOU'LL WANT TO BE SURE YOU ADD ITASCA STATE PARK TO YOUR MINNESOTA ITINERARY.

SIGNIFICANTLY, THE PARK IS A SORT OF ONE-STOP-SHOP FOR OUTDOOR FUN.

WHILE VISITING THE PARK YOU CAN DO THINGS LIKE CAMP, HUNT, SWIM, BOAT, HIKE, FISH, AND EVEN VISIT A FEW NOTEWORTHY HISTORIC ATTRACTIONS.

ESSENTIALLY, ANY WHOLESOME OUTDOOR ACTIVITY YOU CAN IMAGINE CAN BE ENJOYED WITH ITASCA STATE PARK AS YOUR BACKDROP.

ADDRESS: 36750 MAIN PARK DRIVE, PARK RAPIDS, MN 56470, UNITED STATES

PASSPORT STAMPS:

NOTES :

Cathedral of St. Paul

VISTED DATE :   SPRING ◯ SUMMER ◯ FALL ◯ WINTER ◯

WEATHER :   ☀️◯ ⛅◯ 🌧️◯ 🌨️◯ ⛈️◯ 🌬️◯   🌡️ TEMP :

FEE(S) :   RATING : ☆ ☆ ☆ ☆ ☆   WILL I RETURN?   YES / NO

LODGING :   WHO I WENT WITH :

DESCRIPTION / THINGS TO DO :

THE STUNNING CATHEDRAL OF ST. PAUL IS A MUST-SEE WHEN VISITING MINNESOTA. THIS CATHOLIC-CHURCH IS A MAGNIFICENT WORK OF ARCHITECTURE AND ART THAT'S OPEN TO THE PUBLIC EVERY DAY YEAR-ROUND.

ONE OF THE MOST SIGNIFICANT EXAMPLES OF BEAUX-ARTS ARCHITECTURE, THE CONSTRUCTION OF THE CATHEDRAL BEGAN IN 1907.

FROM THERE, THE CATHEDRAL OPENED ITS DOORS FOR ITS FIRST MASS MANY YEARS LATER IN 1915.

A PLACE OF WORSHIP AND A CIVIC LANDMARK, THE CATHEDRAL OF ST. PAUL IS THE HOME PARISH OF NEARLY 1,000 HOUSEHOLDS, BUT ALSO HAS AN ELEMENTAL ROTATING DOOR FOR VISITORS.

DURING THE WEEKDAYS, PUBLIC TOURS AND PILGRIMAGES ARE HOSTED AT THE CATHEDRAL.

DURING A TOUR, VISITORS WILL SPEND ABOUT ONE HOUR TOURING THE PREMISES AND LEARNING ABOUT ITS UNIQUE AND FAMED HISTORY AND ARCHITECTURE.

FINALLY, THE CATHEDRAL HAS A LOVELY GIFT SHOP FROM WHICH VISITORS CAN PURCHASE SOUVENIRS AND RELIGIOUS IDOLS.

THE RELIGIOUS ATTRACTION, LOCATED IN ST. PAUL, MINNESOTA, IS ESPECIALLY RECOMMENDED FOR RELIGIOUS ENTHUSIASTS AND LOVERS OF ARCHITECTURE.

ADDRESS: 239 SELBY AVE, ST PAUL, MN 55102, UNITED STATES

PASSPORT STAMPS:

NOTES :

Tettegouche State Park

VISTED DATE :   SPRING ◯   SUMMER ◯   FALL ◯   WINTER ◯

WEATHER :   ☀◯   ⛅◯   ☁◯   🌨◯   ⛈◯   🌬◯   🌡TEMP :

FEE(S) :   RATING : ☆ ☆ ☆ ☆ ☆   WILL I RETURN?   YES / NO

LODGING :   WHO I WENT WITH :

DESCRIPTION / THINGS TO DO :

THIS MINNESOTA STATE PARK IS LOCATED ON THE SHORES OF LAKE SUPERIOR JUST OFF A STRETCH OF SCENIC HIGHWAY.

OF NOTE, TETTEGOUCHE STATE PARK IS HOME TO FOUR GORGEOUS WATERFALLS ALL DUMPING INTO THE BAPTISM RIVER.

THE PARK HAS MANY SPLENDID LAND WATER FEATURES INCLUDING SEA CAVES, A SEA STACK, AND MORE.

ONE OF THE PARK'S MOST DESIRABLE VIEWS CAN BE SEEN FROM AN OVERLOOK AT SHOVEL POINT.

POOLS AT THE BASE OF THE WATERFALLS ARE IDEAL FOR SWIMMING AS WELL AS NATURAL POOLS ALONG HIGH FALLS TRAIL ALONG THE RIVER.

IN ADDITION TO ALL OF ITS NATURAL FEATURES, TETTEGOUCHE STATE PARK HAS BIKE TRAILS, KAYAK/ CANOE RENTALS, GROOMED CROSS-COUNTRY SKIING, BOAT ACCESS, A GROOMED SNOWMOBILE TRAIL, AND BEYOND.

IN ADDITION TO A DAY TRIP TO THE PARK, YOU COULD ALSO STAY FOR A FEW DAYS ON THE LOVELY CAMPGROUNDS THAT WELCOME TENT- AND RV- CAMPERS BUT THE PARK ALSO HAS SEVERAL CAB-INS FOR RENT AS WELL.

ADDRESS: 5702 MN-61, SILVER BAY, MN 55614, UNITED STATES

PASSPORT STAMPS:

NOTES :

Gooseberry Falls State Park

VISTED DATE :   SPRING ◯ SUMMER ◯ FALL ◯ WINTER ◯

WEATHER :   ☀️◯ ⛅◯ 🌧️◯ 🌨️◯ ⛈️◯ 🌬️◯   🌡️ TEMP :

FEE(S) :   RATING : ☆ ☆ ☆ ☆ ☆   WILL I RETURN? YES / NO

LODGING :   WHO I WENT WITH :

DESCRIPTION / THINGS TO DO :

GOOSEBERRY FALLS STATE PARK, SITUATED ON THE NORTH SHORE OF MINNESOTA, IS KNOWN FOR ITS PICTURESQUE WATERFALLS, A RIVER GORGE, LOG/STONE STRUCTURES, AND WOODSY WILDLIFE.

SIGHTSEEING FOR THE WATERFALLS ALONE IS A BIG DRAW TO THE PARK, BUT THERE'S SO MUCH MORE TO DO IN GOOSEBERRY.

IN THE WINTER MONTHS, THE PARK IS A GREAT PLACE FOR SNOWSHOEING, CROSS-COUNTRY SKIING, AND HIKING. ANY SEASON AT GOOSEBERRY FALLS STATE PARK IS A GOOD SEASON FOR CAMPING.

NOTABLY, THE PARK HAS BOTH TENT AND RV CAMPSITES.

IN ADDITION TO CAMPING AND SNOW RECREATION, THE PARK HAS WONDERFUL AMENITIES SUCH AS PICNIC PAVILIONS, A WARMING CENTER, AND A THEATRE.

THE PARK IS ALSO HOME TO MILES OF BOTH PAVED AND UNPAVED HIKING TRAILS THAT WEAVE IN AND OUT OF THE PARK'S UNIQUE ECOSYSTEM.

A VISITOR'S CENTER, AN INTERPRETIVE EXHIBIT, NATURALIST PROGRAMS, HISTORIC SIGHTS, A GIFT SHOP, AND OTHER FUN AMENITIES ALSO RESIDE IN THE PARK.

ADDRESS: 3206 MN-61, TWO HARBORS, MN 55616, UNITED STATES

PASSPORT STAMPS:

NOTES :

Nickelodeon Universe

VISTED DATE :   SPRING ◯   SUMMER ◯   FALL ◯   WINTER ◯

WEATHER :   ☀ ◯   ⛅ ◯   🌧 ◯   🌨 ◯   ⛈ ◯   🌬 ◯   🌡 TEMP :

FEE(S) :   RATING : ☆ ☆ ☆ ☆ ☆   WILL I RETURN?   YES / NO

LODGING :   WHO I WENT WITH :

DESCRIPTION / THINGS TO DO :

THIS SUPER FUN MINNESOTA ATTRACTION IS AN INDOOR AMUSEMENT PARK HOUSED INSIDE THE MALL OF AMERICA.

WITH FUN ATTRACTIONS AND RIDES THAT ARE ALL NICKELODEON-THEMED, THE PARK IS AN AWESOMELY FUN PLACE TO VISIT WITH CHILDREN. OPEN SEVEN DAYS A WEEK, NICKELODEON UNIVERSE WAS THE WORLD'S FIRST INDOOR AMUSEMENT PARK.

WITH SEVEN ACRES OF ENTERTAINMENT, RIDES, GAMES, AND ATTRACTIONS, THERE IS SOMETHING FUN FOR EVERY AGE LEVEL. FROM ROLLER COASTERS TO RETAIL SHOPS, EVERYONE IN YOUR PARTY WILL HAVE FUN.

IF YOU'RE VISITING THE PARK WITH CHILDREN, YOU'LL WANT TO KNOW THAT THE PARK HAS 12 JUNIOR AND FAMILY RIDES IN ADDITION TO SEVEN EXCITING THRILL RIDES. OTHER FUN ATTRACTIONS INCLUDE BLACKLIGHT MINI-GOLF, AN INDOOR PLAYGROUND, CHARACTER EXPERIENCES, AND MORE.

HOWEVER, ONE OF THE PARK'S MOST LAUDABLE FEATURES IS THAT IT'S A CERTIFIED AUTISM CENTER.

FINALLY, AFTER SPENDING THE AFTERNOON AT THE AMUSEMENT PARK YOU'RE ONLY A HOP, SKIP, AND JUMP AWAY FROM EPIC SHOPPING AND DINING.

ADDRESS: 5000 CENTER CT, BLOOMINGTON, MN 55425, UNITED STATES

PASSPORT STAMPS:

NOTES :

Minnesota Zoo

VISTED DATE :   SPRING ◯   SUMMER ◯   FALL ◯   WINTER ◯

WEATHER : ☀◯ ⛅◯ 🌧◯ 🌨◯ ⛈◯ 🌬◯   🌡TEMP :

FEE(S) :   RATING : ☆ ☆ ☆ ☆ ☆   WILL I RETURN? YES / NO

LODGING :   WHO I WENT WITH :

DESCRIPTION / THINGS TO DO :

LOCATED IN APPLE VALLEY, MINNESOTA ZOO OPENED IN 1978 WITH REVOLUTIONARY DISPLAYS AND APPROACHES.

SITUATED ON NEARLY 500 ACRES, THE ZOO HAS CUTTING-EDGE, WORLD-CLASS EXHIBITS THAT GIVE VISITORS AMAZINGLY IMMERSIVE EXPERIENCES.

THE ZOO OFFERS TONS OF EDUCATIONAL PROGRAMMING THAT TEACHES VISITORS ABOUT UNIQUE WILD ANIMALS, ANIMAL HABITATS, AND SO MUCH MORE.

WITH BOTH LAND, AVIARY, AND AQUATIC ANIMALS ON DISPLAY, MINNESOTA ZOO IS A SPECTACULAR ATTRACTION TO VISIT.

SOME OF THE ZOO'S DELIGHTFUL EXHIBITS FEATURE ANIMALS SUCH AS BATS, TIGERS, HORSES, AND SO MUCH MORE.

OF AQUATIC EXHIBITS, SOME OF THE ANIMALS INCLUDE SHARKS, STINGRAYS, TURTLES, EELS, AND AN ASSORTMENT OF FISH.

LASTLY, THE ZOO HAS A VARIETY OF ENDANGERED ANIMALS LIVING ON THE PROPERTY; SOME OF THESE INCLUDE AFRICAN PENGUINS, BACTRIAN CAMELS, AN AMUR TIGER, AND A BALI MYNAH.

NO MATTER WHICH ANIMALS, EXHIBITS, OR PROGRAMS INTEREST YOU, THERE'S SOMETHING FOR EVERYONE AT MINNESOTA ZOO.

ADDRESS: 13000 ZOO BLVD, APPLE VALLEY, MN 55124, UNITED STATES

PASSPORT STAMPS:

NOTES :

SPAM Museum

WEATHER : ☀ ◯ ⛅ ◯ 🌧 ◯ 🌨 ◯ ⛈ ◯ 💨 ◯   🌡 TEMP :

FEE(S) :   RATING : ☆ ☆ ☆ ☆ ☆   WILL I RETURN? YES / NO

LODGING :   WHO I WENT WITH :

DESCRIPTION / THINGS TO DO :

THIS UNIQUE AND MAYBE ODD MUSEUM IS A FREE ATTRACTION IN AUSTIN, MINNESOTA.

A NOD TO EVERYONE'S FAVORITE CANNED MEAT, SPAM MUSEUM RETELLS THE HISTORY OF HORMEL, MAKER OF SPAM, SPAM ITSELF, AND ITS PLACE IN AMERICANA.

THE 14,000 SQUARE FOOT MUSEUM HAS SEVEN INTERACTIVE, INFORMATIVE, AND ENTERTAINING GALLERIES.

THE MUSEUM HAS IMMERSIVE HANDS-ON DISPLAYS, FUN GAMES, AND INTERESTING VIDEOS.

IF YOU'RE A LOVER OF SPAM, YOU'LL HAVE A BLAST AT THE SPAM MUSEUM.

THE MUSEUM WHICH IS OPEN SEVEN DAYS A WEEK RETELLS THE HISTORY OF THE HORMEL COMPANY AND THE EMERGENCE OF SPAM.

SOME OF THE DISPLAYS FEATURE OLD HORMEL COOKBOOKS, STATUES OF HORMEL BIGWIGS, SPAM PARAPHERNALIA, AND LOTS MORE.

THE MUSEUM ALSO HAS A GREAT GIFT SHOP WHERE YOU CAN PICK UP YOUR FAVORITE SPAM PRODUCTS AS WELL AS UNIQUE SOUVENIRS AND MERCHANDISE.

ADDRESS: 101 3RD AVE NE, AUSTIN, MN 55912, UNITED STATES

PASSPORT STAMPS:

NOTES :

Theodore Wirth Regional Park

VISTED DATE :   SPRING ◯ SUMMER ◯ FALL ◯ WINTER ◯

WEATHER : ☀◯ 🌤◯ 🌧◯ 🌨◯ ⛈◯ 🌬◯   🌡 TEMP :

FEE(S) :   RATING : ☆ ☆ ☆ ☆ ☆   WILL I RETURN?   YES / NO

LODGING :   WHO I WENT WITH :

DESCRIPTION / THINGS TO DO :

THIS NEARLY 800-ACRE PARK LOCATED IN GOLDEN VALLEY, MINNESOTA, IS HOME TO TONS OF YEAR-ROUND RECREATION. ESTABLISHED IN 1889, SOME OF THE PARK'S POPULAR FEATURES INCLUDE LAKE ACTIVITIES AND A CHALET-STYLE CLUBHOUSE.

NAMED FOR THE SUPERINTENDENT OF MN PARKS FROM 1903-1935, THE PARK'S HISTORY IS DIVERSE AND ITS LANDSCAPE EVERCHANGING.

WHEN FIRST ACQUIRED, THEODORE WIRTH REGIONAL PARK ONLY AMOUNTED TO 64 ACRES, HOWEVER, IT'S BEEN IN A CONSISTENT STATE OF DEVELOPMENT AND EVOLUTION SINCE ITS EARLY BEGINNINGS.

ONE OF THE MOST SIGNIFICANT POINTS TO CONSIDER ABOUT THE PARK IS ITS DIVERSE AND PLENTIFUL RECREATIONAL OPPORTUNITIES AND AMENITIES.

OF NOTE, THE PARK FEATURES A DECORATIVE FOUNTAIN, BIKING/HIKING/CROSS-COUNTRY TRAILS, AN ARCHERY COURSE, A BEACH, FISHING, A DISC GOLF COURSE, PLAYGROUNDS, SPORTS COURTS/FIELDS, AND BEYOND.

SOME OF THE PARK'S MANY AMENITIES INCLUDE, BUT ARE NOT LIMITED TO RESTROOMS, PICNIC AREAS, A FISHING PIER, AND ATHLETIC RENTALS. THE PARK'S BEAUTIFUL LANDSCAPE COUPLED WITH ALL OF ITS FUN OPPORTUNITIES MAKES THEODORE WIRTH REGIONAL PARK A MUST-SEE.

ADDRESS: 1301 THEODORE WIRTH PKWY, GOLDEN VALLEY, MN 55422, UNITED STATES

PASSPORT STAMPS:

NOTES :

Sea Life

VISTED DATE :   SPRING ○   SUMMER ○   FALL ○   WINTER ○

WEATHER :   ☀ ○   ⛅ ○   🌧 ○   🌨 ○   ⛈ ○   🌬 ○   🌡 TEMP :

FEE(S) :   RATING : ☆ ☆ ☆ ☆ ☆   WILL I RETURN?   YES / NO

LODGING :   WHO I WENT WITH :

DESCRIPTION / THINGS TO DO :

SEA LIFE IS A PUBLIC MINNESOTA AQUARIUM SITUATED WITHIN THE ICONIC MALL OF AMERICA.

NOTABLY, THE MORE-THAN-ONE-MILLION-GALLON AQUARIUM PROVIDES VISITORS WITH IMMERSIVE EDUCATIONAL OPPORTUNITIES BY BRINGING THEM FACE TO FACE WITH SOME OF THE WORLD'S MOST AMAZING CREATURES.

IN ADDITION TO LEARNING ABOUT SEA LIFE, VISITORS ALSO GET TO EXPLORE AQUATIC ECOSYSTEMS AND ANIMAL HABITATS.

WHETHER VISITING WITH ADULTS, CHILDREN, OR A COMBINATION OF BOTH, SEA LIFE IS A WONDERFUL MINNESOTA ATTRACTION. FURTHERMORE, SOME OF THE CENTER'S EXHIBITS SHOWCASE UNDERWATER TUNNELS, RAINFOREST FEATURES, CORAL CAVES, LIFE IN A LAGOON, AND ROCKPOOLS.

ADDITIONALLY, SOME OF THE AMAZING CREATURES ON DISPLAY INCLUDE SHARKS, STINGRAYS, SAWFISH, TURTLES, GUITAR SHARKS, AND MORE.

SOME OF THE FUN THINGS YOU CAN DO, BESIDES OBSERVING THE DISPLAYS, ARE FEEDING EXPERIENCES, SHOWS, AND EXPERT TALKS.

COLORFUL DISPLAYS, HELPFUL GUIDES AND EXPERTS, IMMERSIVE EXPERIENCES, AND THE PROXIMITY TO THE MALL OF AMERICA, ALL MAKE TOURING SEA LIFE A FUN THING TO DO WHEN YOU'RE IN MINNESOTA.

ADDRESS: ONE, MALL OF AMERICA, 120 EAST BROADWAY EAST SIDE, LEVEL, BLOOMINGTON, MN 55425, UNITED STATES

PASSPORT STAMPS:

NOTES :

Stone Arch Bridge

VISTED DATE :   SPRING ◯   SUMMER ◯   FALL ◯   WINTER ◯

WEATHER :   ☀ ◯ ⛅ ◯ 🌧 ◯ 🌨 ◯ ⛈ ◯ 💨 ◯   🌡 TEMP :

FEE(S) :   RATING : ☆ ☆ ☆ ☆ ☆   WILL I RETURN?   YES / NO

LODGING :   WHO I WENT WITH :

DESCRIPTION / THINGS TO DO :

THIS FORMER RAILROAD BRIDGE CROSSES THE MISSISSIPPI RIVER IN DOWNTOWN MINNEAPOLIS, MN.

THE BEAUTIFUL ARCHED BRIDGE IS MADE ENTIRELY OF HAND-LAID STONE AND OVERLOOKS SAINT ANTHONY FALLS.

THE BRIDGE WAS EXPERTLY CONSTRUCTED IN 1881 AND MEASURES 2,100 FEET IN TOTAL LENGTH AND HAS A TOTAL BOAT CLEARANCE OF JUST OVER 24 FEET.

BESIDES MAKING A GORGEOUS BACKDROP FOR PHOTOGRAPHY, THE STONE ARCH BRIDGE CAN ALSO BE USED FOR RECREATIONAL PURPOSES.

IF YOU'LL BE SPENDING ANY TIME IN MINNEAPOLIS, BE SURE TO CHECK OUT THIS ARCHITECTURALLY ASTOUNDING BRIDGE.

SIGNIFICANTLY, BESIDES BEING A GORGEOUS SIGHT TO SEE, THE BRIDGE IS OPEN TO PEDESTRIAN TRAFFIC FOR WALKING, RUNNING, AND BIKING.

IN FACT, WALKING OR RIDING OVER THE BRIDGE WILL GIVE YOU THE MOST SPECTACULAR VIEWS OF THE MISSISSIPPI RIVER. OBSERVANCE OF THE BRIDGE IS ALSO INTERESTING AS IT'S BEEN DESIGNATED A NATIONAL HISTORIC LANDMARK.

WHETHER YOU ENJOY STROLLING, SKATING, OR BEYOND, YOU'LL SURELY DELIGHT IN THE VIEWS OF AND FROM STONE ARCH BRIDGE.

ADDRESS: 100 PORTLAND AVE, MINNEAPOLIS, MN 55401, UNITED STATES

PASSPORT STAMPS:

NOTES :

Boundary Waters Canoe Area Wilderness

VISTED DATE :   SPRING ○ SUMMER ○ FALL ○ WINTER ○

WEATHER : ☀ ○ ⛅ ○ ☁ ○ 🌨 ○ ⛈ ○ 🌬 ○   🌡 TEMP :

FEE(S) :   RATING : ☆ ☆ ☆ ☆ ☆   WILL I RETURN? YES / NO

LODGING :   WHO I WENT WITH :

DESCRIPTION / THINGS TO DO :

THIS MINNESOTA ATTRACTION IS A MORE-THAN-ONE-MILLION-ACRE WILDERNESS AREA WITHIN THE SUPERIOR NATIONAL FOREST. TRAVELERS FROM THE US AND CANADA FLOCK TO BOUNDARY WATERS CANOE AREA WILDERNESS EACH YEAR.

OF NOTE, THE AREA IS HOME TO SEVERAL EDUCATIONAL RESOURCE CENTERS SUCH AS A NATURE & SCIENCE CENTER, A HISTORY & CULTURE CENTER, AND A KIDS PROGRAM TO NAME A FEW.

THE AREA'S LANDSCAPE IS HOME TO DIVERSE ANIMALS, ECOSYSTEMS, WATER, AND VEGETATION, ALL OF WHICH MAKE EXPLORING THE AREA REMARKABLE. THE BOUNDARY WATERS CANOE AREA WILDE-RNESS ALSO HAS PLENTY OF OPPORTUNITIES FOR OUTDOOR RECREATION.

OF NOTE, VISITORS TO THE PARK CAN ENJOY CAMPING, BIKING, HIKING, CLIMBING, FISHING, HUNTING, AND HORSEBACK RIDING.

ADDITIONALLY, NATURE OBSERVANCE, ROCK COLLECTING, PICNICKING, AND SCENIC DRIVES ARE DRAWS TO THE PARK.

FINALLY, THE AREA IS THE SETTING FOR MANY WATERSPORTS SUCH AS CANOEING, KAYAKING, AND SWIMMING. WHETHER YOU'RE LOOKING TO GET AWAY FROM THE HUBBUB OF DAILY LIFE, IMPROVE YOUR APPRECIATION FOR NATURE, OR JUST LEARN ABOUT THE DIVERSE WILDERNESS, YOU'LL SURELY ENJOY YOUR VISIT TO BOUNDARY WATERS CANOE AREA WILDERNESS.

ADDRESS: DULUTH, MN 55808, UNITED STATES

PASSPORT STAMPS:

NOTES :

Niagara Cave

VISTED DATE :   SPRING ◯ SUMMER ◯ FALL ◯ WINTER ◯

WEATHER : ☀◯ ⛅◯ ☁◯ 🌨◯ ⛈◯ 🌬◯   🌡TEMP :

FEE(S) :   RATING : ☆ ☆ ☆ ☆ ☆   WILL I RETURN? YES / NO

LODGING :   WHO I WENT WITH :

DESCRIPTION / THINGS TO DO :

THIS LIMESTONE CAVE IS SITUATED IN BEAUTIFUL HARMONY, MINNESOTA; ALTHOUGH IT'S PRIVATELY OWNED, TOUR RESERVATIONS CAN BE MADE.

OF NOTE, NIAGARA CAVE IS AN ASTOUNDING 200 FEET DEEP AND IS SURROUNDED BY SURPRISING AND INTERESTING FEATURES.

SOME OF THE AREA'S NOTEWORTHY FEATURES INCLUDE A 60-FOOT WATERFALL, FOSSILS, AN UNDERGROUND STREAM, STALACTITES, AND STALAGMITES.

CAVE TOURS ARE PERFECT FOR FAMILIES AND SUITABLE FOR CHILDREN AS YOUNG AS SIX YEARS OLD.

ONE OF THE MOST EXCITING PARTS OF THE NIAGARA CAVE TOUR IS THE ELEVATOR RIDE TO THE DEPTHS OF THE EARTH. NIAGARA CAVE IS ALSO HOME TO OTHER AWESOME RECREATIONAL ACTIVITIES.

FOR INSTANCE, WHILE VISITING THE CAVES YOU CAN ENJOY THE ON-PROPERTY MINI-GOLF COURSE, GEM PANNING, PICNIC SHELTERS, AND PLAYGROUNDS.

FINALLY, A YUMMY CONCESSION STAND IS ALSO ON THE PROPERTY.

SO, FORGET ABOUT PACKING LUNCH OR PLANNING ACTIVITIES AND HEAD TO NIAGARA CAVE WHERE IT'S ALL PLANNED OUT FOR YOU.

ADDRESS: 29842 CO HWY 30, HARMONY, MN 55939, UNITED STATES

PASSPORT STAMPS:

NOTES :

Temperance River

VISTED DATE :   SPRING ◯   SUMMER ◯   FALL ◯   WINTER ◯

WEATHER :   ☀◯ ⛅◯ 🌧◯ 🌨◯ ⛈◯ 🌬◯   🌡 TEMP :

FEE(S) :   RATING : ☆ ☆ ☆ ☆ ☆   WILL I RETURN?   YES / NO

LODGING :   WHO I WENT WITH :

DESCRIPTION / THINGS TO DO :

THIS NEARLY 40-MILE RIVER IN NORTHERN MINNESOTA DRAINS INTO LAKE SUPERIOR.

FLOWING SOUTH FROM BRULE LAKE IN COOK COUNTY, TEMPERANCE RIVER WAS IRONICALLY NAMED FOR THE STRONG WATER FLOW THAT IMPEDES DEBRIS BUILD-UP AT ITS MOUTH.

MANY SPOTS ALONG THE RIVER'S STRETCH ARE SUITABLE FOR FISHING WHILE OBSTACLES IN SOME PARTS PREVENT FISHING. THE PARK SURROUNDING THE RIVER IS RIFE WITH NATURE TRAILS AND OBSERVANCE OPPORTUNITIES.

ALTHOUGH PERMITTED IN MANY PARTS OF THE PARK, PETS ARE ALLOWED EXCEPT IN DESIGNATED SWIMMING AREAS OF WHICH THERE ARE MANY.

SURROUNDING THE TEMPERANCE RIVER ARE WONDERFUL OPPORTUNITIES FOR CAMPING AS WELL.

OTHER RIVER AREA FEATURES INCLUDE WATERFALLS, ROCK CLIMBING, PICNIC AREAS, AND MANY SNOW SPORTS. ROCK FORMATIONS SURROUNDING THE RIVER RISE 900 FEET HIGH WHICH INTRODUCE YOU TO BREATHTAKING VIEWS.

MOREOVER, 22 MILES WORTH OF HIKING TRAILS RUN RIVERSIDE LEADING TO LAKE SUPERIOR.

FINALLY, VISITORS TO TEMPERANCE RIVER ARE WELCOMED BY A LOVELY VISITOR CENTER THAT ALSO HOUSES A NATURE STORE.

ADDRESS: 7620 WEST, MN-61, SCHROEDER, MN 55613, UNITED STATES

PASSPORT STAMPS:

NOTES :

Lake Minnetonka

VISTED DATE :   SPRING ◯ SUMMER ◯ FALL ◯ WINTER ◯

WEATHER :   ☀ ◯ ⛅ ◯ 🌧 ◯ 🌨 ◯ ⛈ ◯ 🌬 ◯   🌡 TEMP :

FEE(S) :   RATING : ☆ ☆ ☆ ☆ ☆   WILL I RETURN? YES / NO

LODGING :   WHO I WENT WITH :

DESCRIPTION / THINGS TO DO :

LOCATED ROUGHLY 15 MILES WEST OF MINNEAPOLIS, MN, LAKE MINNETONKA IS MADE UP OF A SERIES OF INTERCONNECTING LAKES AND OTHER SURROUNDING WATERWAYS.

VAST IN SIZE, THE LAKE RESIDES IN TWO LARGE COUNTIES AND HAS A SHORE LENGTH OF MORE THAN 120 MILES.

MINNETONKA'S LAKESIDE IS HOME TO MANY EXCITING ATTRACTIONS WHILE THE LAKE ITSELF SERVES AS AN EXCELLENT PLACE TO EXPLORE AND PARTAKE IN WATER SPORTS.

SOME OF THE FUN ATTRACTIONS SITUATED NEAR THE LAKE INCLUDE A ROLLER COASTER, AN AQUARIUM, AND AN AVIARY.

ADDITIONALLY, THE LAKE AREA HAS AN ECLECTIC SHOPPING, DINING, AND ENTERTAINMENT SCENE.

SOME OF LAKE MINNETONKA'S WATER ACTIVITIES FEATURE DINNER CRUISES, BOAT LAUNCHES, A PLAY-HOUSE, A DINNER THEATRE, A TROLLEY SYSTEM, BOAT RACES, GARDENS, CAMPING, AND LOADS MORE.

LASTLY, THE LAKE'S SURROUNDING AREA HAS AWESOME HIKING TRAILS AND EXCELLENT CAMPSITES.

A VISIT TO LAKE MINNETONKA IS A WONDERFUL TOURIST ATTRACTION THAT YOU WON'T WANT TO MISS.

ADDRESS: MN, UNITED STATES

PASSPORT STAMPS:

NOTES :

Pipestone National Monument

VISTED DATE :   SPRING ◯   SUMMER ◯   FALL ◯   WINTER ◯

WEATHER :   ☀◯ 🌤◯ ☁◯ 🌨◯ ⛈◯ 💨◯   🌡 TEMP :

FEE(S) :   RATING : ☆ ☆ ☆ ☆ ☆   WILL I RETURN?   YES / NO

LODGING :   WHO I WENT WITH :

DESCRIPTION / THINGS TO DO :

LOCATED JUST NORTH OF PIPESTONE, MN, THE PIPESTONE NATIONAL MONUMENT IS SITUATED IN THE SOUTHWESTERN PART OF THE STATE.

CREATED IN 1937 BY ORDER OF CONGRESS, THE MONUMENT SIGNIFIES RESPECT AND HONOR OF INDIGENOUS PEOPLES.

SPECIFICALLY, THE MONUMENT IS AN AREA OF ARCHAEOLOGICAL, ETHNIC, AND HISTORICAL IMPORTANCE THAT CELEBRATES THE CONTRIBUTIONS MADE TO THE AREA BY NATIVE AMERICANS.

THE MONUMENT IS STUNNINGLY SET IN A NATURAL PRAIRIE SETTING THAT PAYS HOMAGE TO THE LAND'S NATURAL BEAUTY AND THE NATIVE'S RESPECT FOR IT.

THE MONUMENT RECEIVED ITS NAME SPECIFICALLY TO HONOR THE THOUSANDS OF NATIVE AMERICANS WHO HAVE QUARRIED THE NATURALLY OCCURRING PIPESTONE NATIVE TO THE AREA.

THIS LAND IS CONSIDERED HOLY BY THE NATIVES WHO HAVE INCLUDED THE QUARRIED PIPESTONE IN THE SAME PIPES THEY USE TO PRAY.

TRAVELERS TO THE GOPHER STATE CAN TOUR THE QUARRIES AND LOOK FOR PIPESTONE AS WELL AS REVEL AT THE REVERED PIPESTONE NATIONAL MONUMENT.

ADDRESS: 36 RESERVATION AVE, PIPESTONE, MN 56164, UNITED STATES

PASSPORT STAMPS:

NOTES :

Museum of Questionable Medical Devices

VISTED DATE :   SPRING ◯   SUMMER ◯   FALL ◯   WINTER ◯

WEATHER : ☀️◯   ⛅◯   ☁️◯   🌧️◯   ⛈️◯   🌬️◯   🌡️TEMP :

FEE(S) :   RATING : ☆ ☆ ☆ ☆ ☆   WILL I RETURN?   YES / NO

LODGING :   WHO I WENT WITH :

DESCRIPTION / THINGS TO DO :

HOUSED WITHIN THE SCIENCE MUSEUM OF MINNESOTA SITS THE COLLECTIONS OF THE FORMER MUSEUM OF QUESTIONABLE MEDICAL DEVICES.

ONCE AN ESTABLISHMENT IN AND OF ITSELF, THE MUSEUM OF QUESTIONABLE MEDICAL DEVICES' DOORS CLOSED IN 2002 AND IT WAS RELOCATED AS A LARGE COLLECTION WITHIN THE SCIENCE MUSEUM.

ESSENTIALLY, THE MUSEUM IS NOW A MUSEUM WITHIN A MUSEUM.

NONETHELESS, THE ARTIFACTS OF THIS COLLECTION PAINT STRANGE AND DOWNRIGHT CRIMINAL STORIES FROM THE WORLD OF MEDICINE.

WHEN VISITING THIS INTERESTING PLACE, YOU WILL BE TREATED TO ODD AND CURIOUS MEDICAL DOCUMENTS, RELICS, STORIES, AND MORE.

DUBIOUS MEDICAL DEVICES, FRIGHTENING MACHINES, MIND-BLOWING SOAPS/BALMS, GADGETS, AND MORE ARE ALL HOUSED WITHIN THE MUSEUM.

THEY TELL STRANGE STORIES OF PSEUDOSCIENCE THAT ARE ALMOST TOO UNBELIEVABLE TO BE TRUE.

IF YOU HAVE A PENCHANT FOR ODDITIES, YOU WON'T WANT TO MISS OUT ON THE MUSEUM OF QUESTIONABLE MEDICAL DEVICES.

ADDRESS: 120 W KELLOGG BOULEVARD, SAINT PAUL, MN 55102, UNITED STATES

PASSPORT STAMPS:

NOTES :

Minnesota's Largest Candy Store

VISTED DATE :   SPRING ◯   SUMMER ◯   FALL ◯   WINTER ◯

WEATHER :   ☀️◯   ⛅◯   ☁️◯   🌨️◯   ⛈️◯   🌬️◯   🌡️TEMP :

FEE(S) :   RATING : ☆ ☆ ☆ ☆ ☆   WILL I RETURN?   YES / NO

LODGING :   WHO I WENT WITH :

DESCRIPTION / THINGS TO DO :

IF YOU OR ANYONE IN YOUR TRAVEL GROUP HAVE A SWEET TOOTH, YOU WON'T WANT TO MISS OUT ON THIS ICONIC MN LOCALE.

A GOLDEN-DOMED, BRIGHT YELLOW RETAIL HAVEN, MINNESOTA'S LARGEST CANDY STORE IS A SIGHT TO BEHOLD. FAMILY-OWNED AND OPERATED FOR NEARLY 40 YEARS, THE ESTABLISHMENT IS A MUCH-LOVED PURVEYOR OF SWEETS.

WITH INSANE VARIETIES OF CANDIES, CONFECTIONS, SODA POP, AND BEYOND, YOU WON'T KNOW WHICH WAY TO LOOK AS YOU MEANDER THE STORE.

IN ADDITION TO SHOPPING FOR SWEETS GALORE, THE UNIQUE AND BRIGHTLY COLORED ART AND ARCHITECTURE OF THE SHOP ARE ENJOYABLE TO PERUSE.

CHILDREN AND ADULTS ARE MESMERIZED BY PAINTED CEILINGS AND WHIMSICAL SCENES AS WELL AS FOOD AND POP CULTURE IMPRESSIONS.

MOREOVER, A HUGE BILLBOARD OVERLOOKS THE SHOP'S EXIT AND ITSELF IS A LANDMARK VISITORS' ATTRACTION. NOTABLY, IT USUALLY DONS SOME WITTY PUN OR IRONIC JUDGMENT.

ONE OF THE COUNTLESS UNIQUE PLACES IN THE GOPHER STATE, BE SURE TO MAKE TIME FOR A PITSTOP AT MINNESOTA'S LARGEST CANDY STORE.

ADDRESS: 20430 JOHNSON MEMORIAL DR, JORDAN, MN 55352, UNITED STATES

PASSPORT STAMPS:

NOTES :

Bear Head Lake State Park

VISTED DATE :   SPRING ◯ SUMMER ◯ FALL ◯ WINTER ◯

WEATHER : ☀️◯ ⛅◯ 🌧️◯ ❄️◯ ⛈️◯ 🌬️◯   🌡️TEMP :

FEE(S) :   RATING : ☆ ☆ ☆ ☆ ☆   WILL I RETURN? YES / NO

LODGING :   WHO I WENT WITH :

DESCRIPTION / THINGS TO DO :

BEAR HEAD LAKE STATE PARK IS ONE OF MINNESOTA'S MOST POPULAR OUTDOOR RECREATIONAL AREAS.

IT'S GOT STUNNING SCENIC VIEWS TO TAKE IN, NOT UNLIKE ONES YOU'LL COME ACROSS IN THE NEARBY BOUNDARY WATERS CANOE AREA WILDERNESS.

THE MOST POPULAR VISITOR ACTIVITIES ARE HIKING, FISHING, SWIMMING, AND BOATING ON THE 5,540-ACRE PROPERTY.

THE PARK HAS BEEN VOTED "AMERICA'S FAVORITE PARK" IN THE PAST, AND RIGHTLY SO BECAUSE THERE IS SO MUCH THERE FOR VISITORS OF ALL AGES TO SEE AND DO.

DURING THE SUMMER, PEOPLE COME FROM FAR AND WIDE TO TAKE A DIP IN THEIR SANDY SWIMMING BEACH, BUT OTHER THINGS YOU CAN DO ALSO INCLUDE CANOEING, SNOWSHOEING, AND CROSS-COUNTRY SKIING.

ADDRESS: 9301 BEAR HEAD STATE PARK ROAD, ELY, MN 55731,US

PASSPORT STAMPS:

NOTES :

Blue Mounds State Park

VISTED DATE :   SPRING ◯ SUMMER ◯ FALL ◯ WINTER ◯

WEATHER : ☀️◯ ⛅◯ 🌧️◯ 🌨️◯ ⛈️◯ 🌬️◯   🌡️TEMP :

FEE(S) :   RATING : ☆ ☆ ☆ ☆ ☆   WILL I RETURN? YES / NO

LODGING :   WHO I WENT WITH :

DESCRIPTION / THINGS TO DO :

LOCATED NEAR THE TOWN OF LUVERNE, BLUE MOUNDS STATE PARK IS NAMED AFTER AN ESCARPMENT OF PRECAMBRIAN SIOUX QUARTZITE BEDROCK.

THOUGH THE STRUCTURE IS MORE PINK, IT APPEARED TO BE BLUE TO EARLY SETTLERS WHO SAW IT FROM A DISTANCE.

ONE OF THE MOST POPULAR ACTIVITIES IN THE PARK IS ROCK CLIMBING; OTHER THINGS YOU CAN DO ALSO INCLUDE SWIMMING IN THE SMALL RESERVOIR OR VISITING THE PARK'S INTERPRETIVE CENTER WHICH WAS ONCE THE HOME OF AUTHOR FREDERICK MANFRED.

ANOTHER UNIQUE ASPECT OF THE PARK IS THAT IT PROTECTS A HERD OF AMERICAN BISON, WHICH GRAZES THERE ON A LARGE PRAIRIE REMNANT.

ADDRESS: 1410 161ST ST, LUVERNE, MN 56156, UNITED STATES

PASSPORT STAMPS:

NOTES :

Cascade River State Park

VISTED DATE : SPRING ◯ SUMMER ◯ FALL ◯ WINTER ◯

WEATHER : ☀ ◯ ⛅ ◯ 🌧 ◯ 🌨 ◯ ⛈ ◯ 💨 ◯ 🌡 TEMP :

FEE(S) : RATING : ☆ ☆ ☆ ☆ ☆ WILL I RETURN? YES / NO

LODGING : WHO I WENT WITH :

DESCRIPTION / THINGS TO DO :

CASCADE RIVER STATE PARK CAN BE FOUND ON THE NORTHERN SHORE OF LAKE SUPERIOR; BECAUSE OF ITS RUGGED AND ROCKY LOCATION, YOU'LL BE SURE TO COME ACROSS A DIVERSE VARIETY OF FLORA AND FAUNA WHILE YOU'RE THERE.

SOME OF THE THINGS PEOPLE LIKE TO DO DURING THEIR VISIT ARE EXPLORE AND PHOTOGRAPH THE SCENIC AREAS ALONG THE LAKE AND RIVER, GO FISHING, WET THEIR FEET IN THE WATERFALLS, OR ENJOY THEMSELVES WHILE HIKING OR CAMPING.

THERE ARE SEVEN PICNIC SITES IN THE PARK, ONE OF WHICH IS UNDER A GROVE OF CEDAR TREES AND IS ONE OF THE MOST BEAUTIFUL SPOTS IN THE ENTIRE PARK.

ADDRESS: WEST, 3481 MINNESOTA 61, LUTSEN, MN 55612, UNITED STATES

PASSPORT STAMPS:

NOTES :

Frontenac State Park

VISTED DATE :   SPRING ◯   SUMMER ◯   FALL ◯   WINTER ◯

WEATHER : ☀◯ ⛅◯ 🌧◯ 🌨◯ ⛈◯ 🌬◯   🌡TEMP :

FEE(S) :   RATING : ☆ ☆ ☆ ☆ ☆   WILL I RETURN? YES / NO

LODGING :   WHO I WENT WITH :

DESCRIPTION / THINGS TO DO :

SINCE 1957 FRONTENAC STATE PARK HAS BEEN A POPULAR PLACE FOR VISITORS TO SPEND THE DAY OUTDOORS.

THE PARK IS MOST RECOGNIZED FOR ITS RICH AND DIVERSE HISTORY AS WELL AS AN AMAZING BIRD WATCHING SITE SINCE IT HOUSES AN ARRAY OF RESIDENTIAL AND MIGRATORY BIRD SPECIES.

THERE ARE SEVERAL TRAILS YOU CAN HIKE THROUGH, MANY OF THEM WHICH LOOP FOR A PERFECT EXPLORATORY OPPORTUNITY;

THE TRAILS ARE GROOMED FOR SNOWMOBILING AND CROSS-COUNTRY SKIING DURING THE WINTER SEASON.

OTHER RECREATIONAL ACTIVITIES AVAILABLE THERE ARE CAMPING, SLEDDING, SWIMMING, AND FISHING FOR CHANNEL CATFISH, NORTHERN PIKE, BLUEGILL, CRAPPIE, AND OTHER FISH IN LAKE PEPIN.

ADDRESS: 29223 COUNTY 28 BLVD, FRONTENAC, MN 55026, UNITED STATES

PASSPORT STAMPS:

NOTES :

Glacial Lakes State Park

VISTED DATE :   SPRING ◯   SUMMER ◯   FALL ◯   WINTER ◯

WEATHER :   ☀ ◯   ⛅ ◯   🌧 ◯   🌨 ◯   ⛈ ◯   🌬 ◯   🌡 TEMP :

FEE(S) :   RATING : ☆ ☆ ☆ ☆ ☆   WILL I RETURN?   YES / NO

LODGING :   WHO I WENT WITH :

DESCRIPTION / THINGS TO DO :

GLACIAL LAKES STATE PARK WAS FOUNDED IN 1963 AS A MEANS OF PRESERVING SOME OF THE REMAINING ROLLING PRAIRIE, WHICH CAN'T BE FOUND A LOT THESE DAYS, BUT ONCE COVERED MUCH OF THE STATE.

THE PARK AND THE SURROUNDING AREA CONTAIN MANY GLACIAL LANDFORMS BECAUSE OF ITS LOCATION NEAR THE WISCONSINAN GLACIATION.

LOCATED IN THE LEAF MOUNTAINS, THE 2,423-ACRE PARK IS FILLED WITH FLORA AND FAUNA THAT RESIDE IN THE WOODLANDS AND PRAIRIES.

OTHER THAN WILDLIFE VIEWING, YOU'LL ALSO BE ABLE TO GO BOATING, FISHING, SWIMMING, SNOWSHOEING, SNOWMOBILING, AND CROSS-COUNTRY SKIING.

STARGAZING IS ALSO EXTREMELY POPULAR AT THE PARK BECAUSE OF ITS REMOTE LOCATION WITH LOW LIGHT POLLUTION.

ADDRESS: 25022 CO RD 41, STARBUCK, MN 56381, UNITED STATES

PASSPORT STAMPS:

NOTES :

Grand Portage State Park

VISTED DATE :   SPRING ◯ SUMMER ◯ FALL ◯ WINTER ◯

WEATHER : ☀️◯ 🌤️◯ 🌧️◯ 🌨️◯ ⛈️◯ 💨◯   🌡️TEMP :

FEE(S) :   RATING : ☆ ☆ ☆ ☆ ☆   WILL I RETURN? YES / NO

LODGING :   WHO I WENT WITH :

DESCRIPTION / THINGS TO DO :

ESTABLISHED IN 1989, GRAND PORTAGE STATE PARK IS A 278-ACRE OUTDOOR SPACE THAT CAN BE FOUND RIGHT ALONGSIDE THE CANADA - UNITED STATES BORDER.

IT IS THE ONLY U.S. STATE PARK THAT IS JOINTLY MANAGED BY A STATE AS WELL AS THE GRAND PORTAGE INDIAN RESERVATION.

THE FIRST DESTINATION VISITORS USUALLY GO TO WHEN THEY ARE IN THE PARK IS USUALLY EITHER HIGH FALLS OR MIDDLE FALLS; HIGH FALLS IS A POPULAR OPTION WITH MANY BECAUSE THE TRAIL IS PAVED AND HAS A BOARDWALK WHICH LEADS DIRECTLY TO THE FALLS, MAKING IT ACCESSIBLE BY WHEELCHAIR.

OTHER ACTIVITIES YOU CAN PARTICIPATE IN ARE EXPLORING THE MONUMENT AND THE HISTORIC GARDENS, LEARNING ALL ABOUT THE OJIBWE, OR GETTING UP CLOSE AND PERSONAL WITH THE FLORA AND FAUNA THAT CAN BE FOUND THERE.

ADDRESS: 9393 MN-61, GRAND PORTAGE, MN 55605, GA 31401, UNITED STATES

PASSPORT STAMPS:

NOTES :

Made in the USA
Las Vegas, NV
02 December 2022

61017224R00059